Horses in Origamı

Other books by John Montroll
www.johnmontroll.com

General Origami

Origami Worldwide
Teach Yourself Origami: Second Revised Edition
Christmas Origami
Storytime Origami

Animal Origami

Origami Birds
Origami Gone Wild
Dinosaur Origami
Origami Dinosaurs for Beginners
Mythological Creatures and the Chinese Zodiac Origami
Origami Under the Sea
Sea Creatures in Origami
Origami for the Enthusiast
Animal Origami for the Enthusiast

Geometric Origami

Origami and Math: Simple to Complex
Classic Polyhedra Origami
A Constellation of Origami Polyhedra

Dollar Bill Origami

Dollar Bill Animals in Origami
Dollar Bill Origami
Easy Dollar Bill Origami

Simple Origami

Fun and Simple Origami: 101 Easy-to-Fold Projects
Super Simple Origami
Easy Dollar Bill Origami
Easy Origami

Horses in Origami

John Montroll

Dover Publications, Inc.
New York

To Matt, Barbara, Ashley, and Abby

Bibliographical Note

Horses in Origami is a new work, first published
by Dover Publications, Inc., in 2013.

Library of Congress Cataloging-in-Publication Data

Montroll, John.
 Horses in origami / John Montroll.
   pages cm
 ISBN-13: 978-0-486-49960-4
 ISBN-10: 0-486-49960-X
 1. Origami. 2. Horses in art. I. Title.
 TT872.5.M65   2013
 736'.982–dc23   2013009205

Manufactured in the United States by Courier Corporation
49960X01   2013
www.doverpublications.com

Introduction

It is wonderful to dedicate an entire origami book to horses. The noble horse has been a most revered loyal friend. From being a simple pet to a favored mode of transportation, a carrier of tools and belongings to a fierce tool of war, part of the recreational lives of its owners, not to mention the towns and cities around it, the horse has been with humans for thousands of years.

Here is a collection of 26 origami horse-themed models. Several origami artists contributed their designs, showing a wide range of style, expression, and wit, all honoring the spirited horse. And several are my original designs. Models are arranged in groups of *Objects*, such as a pop-up horse card, *General* horses, including many of the contributors work, *Fantasy*, and several *Horse Breeds*.

The contributors are Sy Chen, Evi Binzinger, Hatori Koshiro, Seo Won Seon, Robert J. Lang, Davor Vinko, Fabian Correa G., Gen Hagiwara, Jacky Chan, Román Díaz, and Peter Budai. From USA, South America, Europe, and Asia, they each sent me diagrams, which I modified for a unified style. They each folded and photographed their work which has added much life to this collection.

Each model is accompanied with a photograph and description of the model or horse-related information. The models vary in style and complexity though none are too complex. Each model can be folded from a single square sheet of origami paper. Several of the designs highlight the two sides of origami paper with color and white. The colorful bookmark by Evi Binzinger is a wonderful example. Color effects are also used in Jacky Chan's pegasus and Román Díaz's unicorn.

The diagrams are drawn in the internationally approved Randlett-Yoshizawa style, which is easy to follow once you have learned the basic folds. You can use any kind of square paper for these models, but the best results can be achieved using standard origami paper, which is colored on one side and white on the other. In these diagrams, the shading represents the colored side. Large sheets are easier to use than small ones. Origami supplies can be found in arts and craft shops, or at Dover Publications online: www.doverpublications.com. You can also visit OrigamiUSA at www.origamiusa.org for origami supplies and other related information including an extensive list of local, national, and international origami groups.

Many people helped to make this book possible. Great thanks go to the contributors who supplied diagrams and photographs of their work. I thank Yanktoro Udoumoh for photographing all of my models. I thank my editor, Charley Montroll. I thank Robert J. Lang for helping with the computer. I thank Himanshu Agrawal for his continued support and help in several ways.

John Montroll

www.johnmontroll.com

Contents

★ Simple
★★ Intermediate
★★★ Complex
★★★★ Very Complex

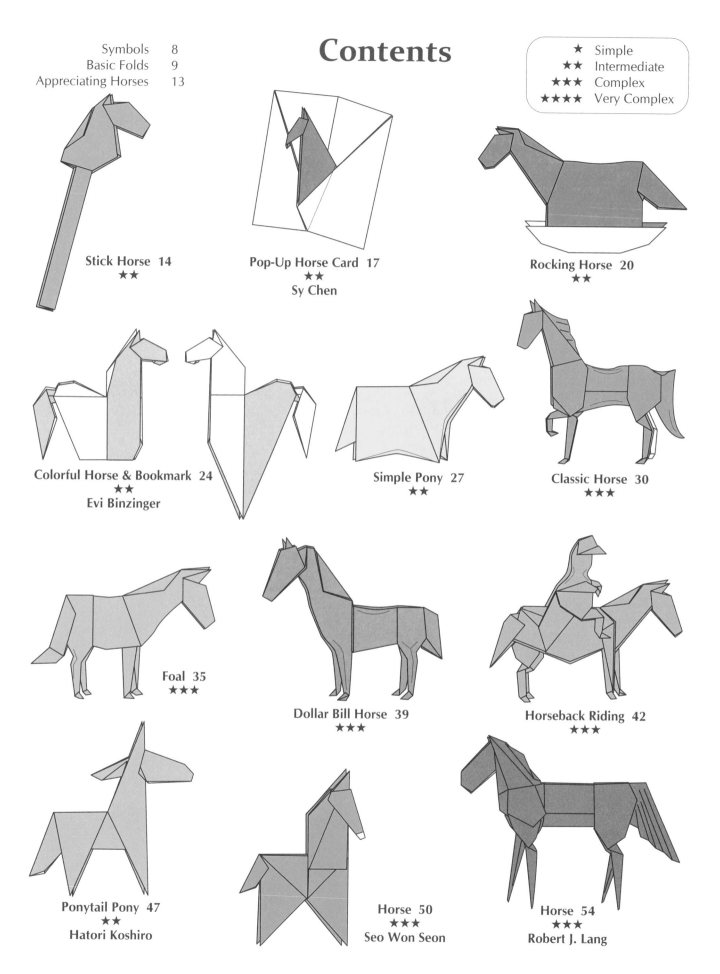

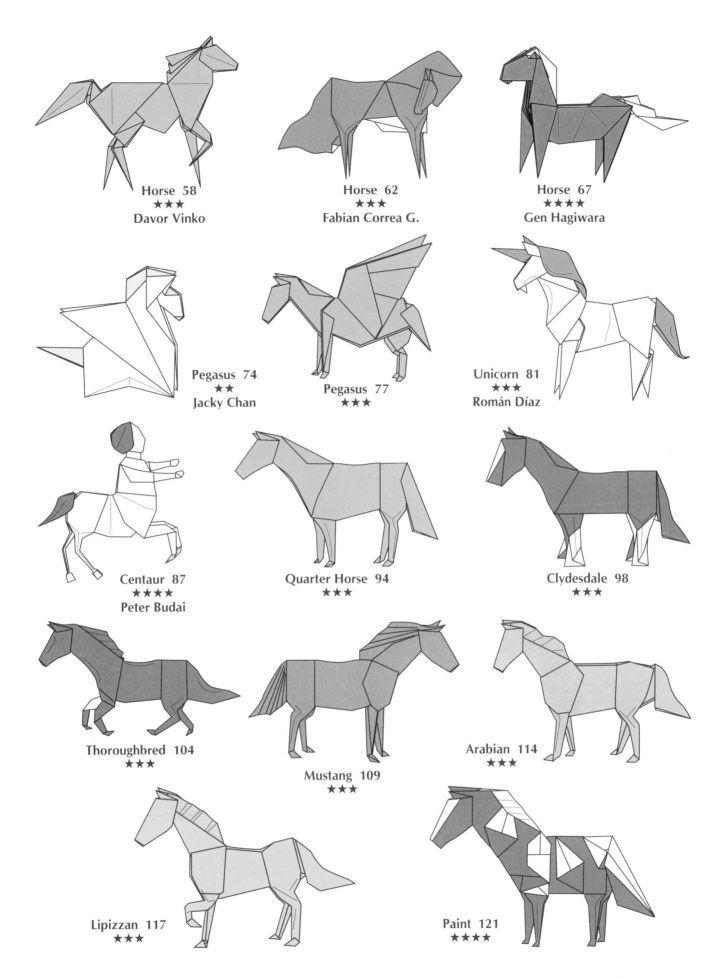

Symbols

Lines

— — — — — — — —   Valley fold, fold in front.

— · — · · — · · — · —   Mountain fold, fold behind.

—————————   Crease line.

·················   X-ray or guide line.

Arrows

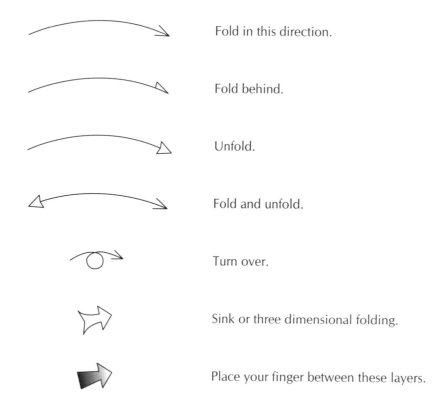

Fold in this direction.

Fold behind.

Unfold.

Fold and unfold.

Turn over.

Sink or three dimensional folding.

Place your finger between these layers.

Basic Folds

Pleat Fold.

Fold back and forth. Each pleat is composed of one valley and mountain fold. Here are two examples.

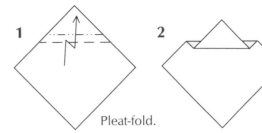

Pleat-fold.

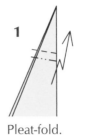

Pleat-fold.

Squash Fold.

In a squash fold, some paper is opened and then made flat. The shaded arrow shows where to place your finger.

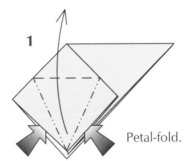

Squash-fold.

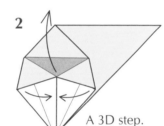

A 3D step.

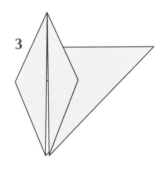

Petal Fold.

In a petal fold, one point is folded up while two opposite sides meet each other.

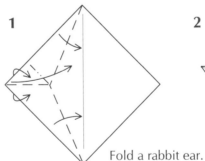

Petal-fold.

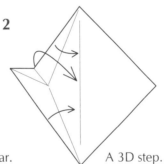

A 3D step.

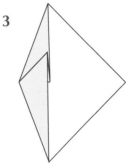

Rabbit Ear.

To fold a rabbit ear, one corner is folded in half and laid down to a side.

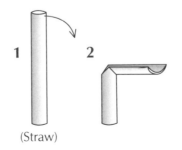

Fold a rabbit ear.

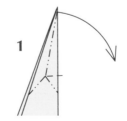

A 3D step.

Double Rabbit Ear.

If you were to bend a straw you would be folding the double rabbit ear.

(Straw)

Double-rabbit-ear.

Inside Reverse Fold.

In an inside reverse fold, some paper is folded between layers. Here are two examples.

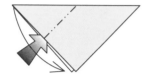 

Reverse-fold.

 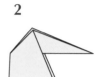

Reverse-fold.

Outside Reverse Fold.

Much of the paper must be unfolded to make an outside reverse fold.

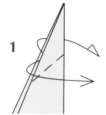

Outside-reverse-fold.

Crimp Fold.

A crimp fold is a combination of two reverse folds. Open the model slightly to form the crimp evenly on each side. Here are two examples.

Crimp-fold.

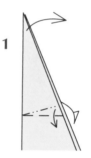 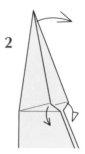 

Crimp-fold.   A 3D step.

Sink.

For a sink, some of the paper without edges is folded inside. To do this fold, much of the model must be unfolded.

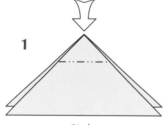 

Sink.

Spread Squash Fold.

A cross between a squash fold and sink fold, some paper in the center is spread apart and then made flat.

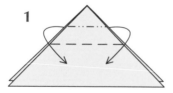 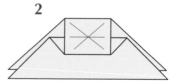

Spread-squash-fold.

Preliminary Fold.

The Preliminary Fold is the starting point for many models. The maneuver in step 3 occurs in many other models.

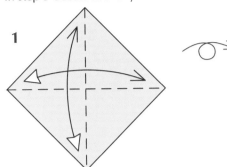

1 Fold and unfold.

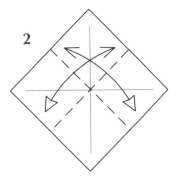

2 Fold and unfold.

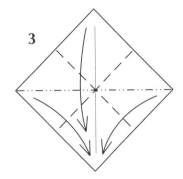

3 Collapse the square by bringing the four corners together.

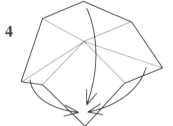

4 This is 3D.

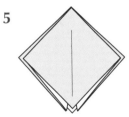

5 Preliminary Fold

Bird Base.

Historically, the Bird Base has been a very popular starting point. The folds used in it occur in many models.

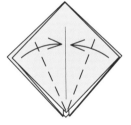

1 Begin with the Preliminary Fold. Kite-fold, repeat behind.

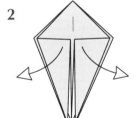

2 Unfold, repeat behind.

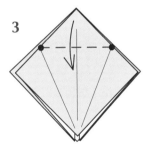

3

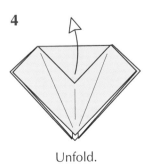

4 Unfold.

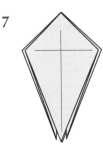

5 Petal-fold, repeat behind.

6 Repeat behind.

7 Bird Base

Blintz Frog Base.

This uses the double unwrap fold which is shown in detail below.

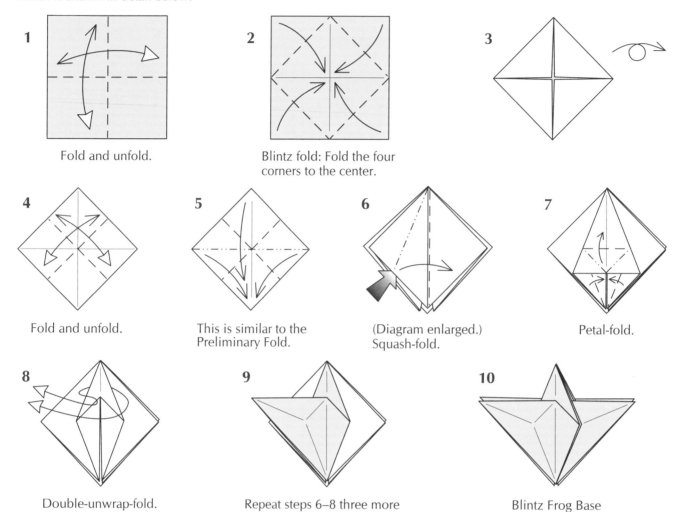

1 Fold and unfold.

2 Blintz fold: Fold the four corners to the center.

3

4 Fold and unfold.

5 This is similar to the Preliminary Fold.

6 (Diagram enlarged.) Squash-fold.

7 Petal-fold.

8 Double-unwrap-fold.

9 Repeat steps 6–8 three more times, on the back and sides.

10 Blintz Frog Base

Double Unwrap Fold.

In the double unwrap fold, locked layers are unwrapped and refolded. Much of the folding is 3D. The diagrams are depicted as shown in steps 8 and 9 of the Blintz Frog Base.

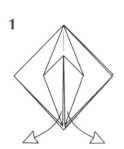

1 Begin with step 8 of the Blintz Frog Base. Spread at the bottom.

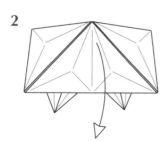

2 Unfold the top layer.

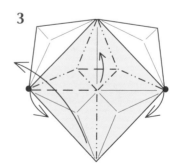

3 Refold along the creases. The dots will meet at the bottom.

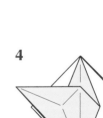

4

Appreciating Horses

Horses are majestic, spirited, powerful, graceful, athletic, potentially gentle animals that have captured the minds and hearts of people for thousands of years. As people have changed the horse through selective breeding for different needs, the horse made a huge impact on civilization.

Horses were used in warfare throughout history. People with these powerful creatures developed battle strategies that gave them the winning advantage. Horses pulled chariots during the bronze and iron ages. Knights in shining armor rode horses in the Middle Ages. For a thousand years, Japanese Samurai used horses. Cavalry was important in the American Civil War.

Horses were used for transportation. Until motorized vehicles, the horse was the quickest way for people to travel with their possessions. Whether horseback riding, or on a horse-drawn carriage, cultures depended on horses for travel and trade.

Horses were used for work. They aided in agriculture by pulling plows, herding cattle, and various other heavy tasks. Goods were placed on horse carts to be wheeled through streets to markets, warehouses, factories, and houses.

Equestrian sports include horse racing, polo, fox hunting, show jumping, rodeo events, horseback riding, and more. Dressage (or Horse Ballet) is a difficult sport where horse and rider are judged on graceful movements.

Today they are not needed for war, transportation, or heavy farm work, though they are still used for smaller jobs. We mainly enjoy them in leisure for companionship and recreation. Throughout the ages, these wonderful creatures have been indispensable to us.

Objects

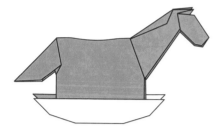

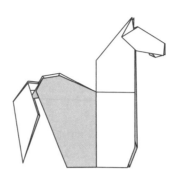

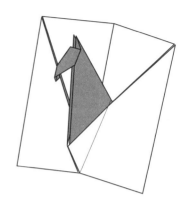

From the playful Rocking Horse to the unique Pop-up Horse Card, this section contains a collection of horse-themed objects.

Stick Horse

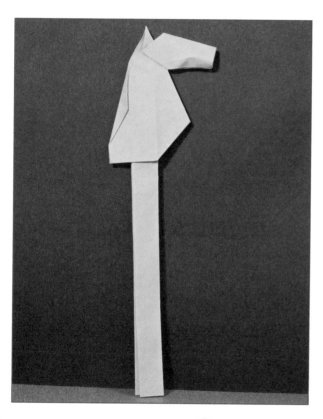

Designed by John Montroll

The stick horse, a simple toy that has captured the imagination of children for generations, has actually been popular since ancient Roman times. Children of all ages still use the stick horse to play pretend in the form of horse racing, rodeo games, jumping contests and fighting the bad guys. Now the collector can add an origami version.

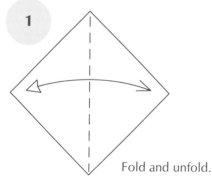

1 Fold and unfold.

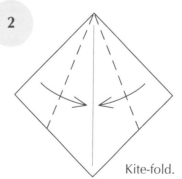

2 Kite-fold.

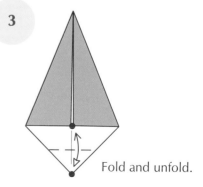

3 Fold and unfold.

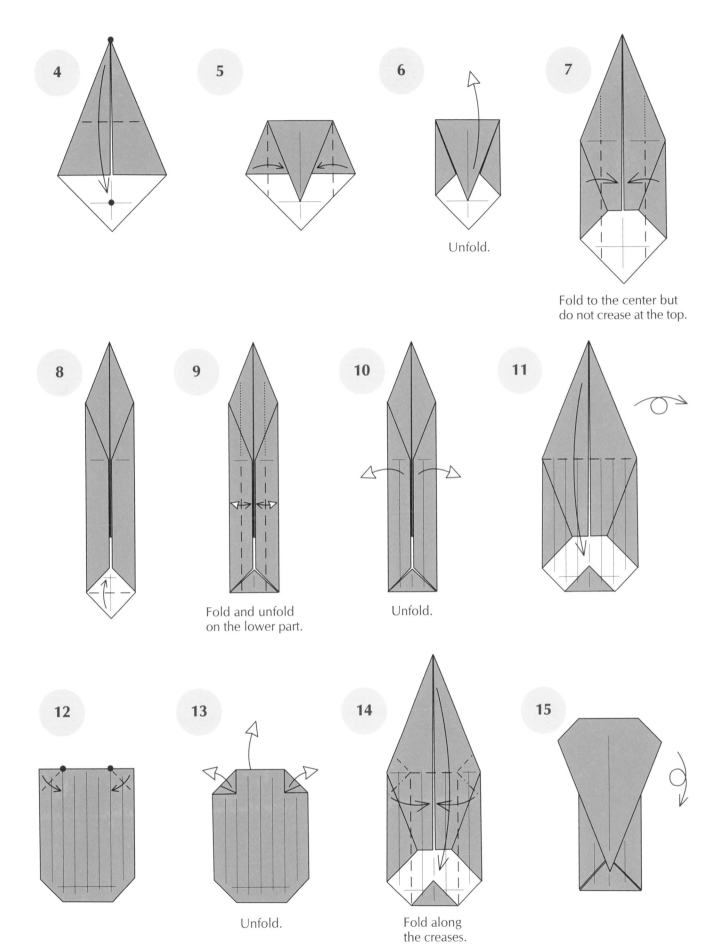

7 Fold to the center but do not crease at the top.

6 Unfold.

9 Fold and unfold on the lower part.

10 Unfold.

13 Unfold.

14 Fold along the creases.

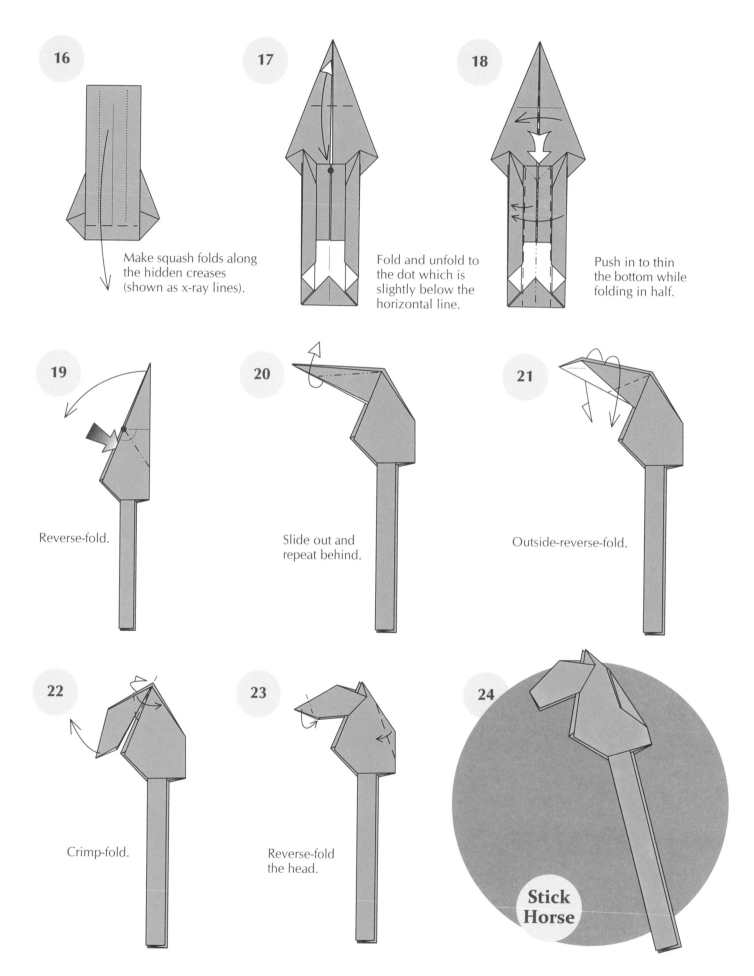

16

Make squash folds along the hidden creases (shown as x-ray lines).

17

Fold and unfold to the dot which is slightly below the horizontal line.

18

Push in to thin the bottom while folding in half.

19

Reverse-fold.

20

Slide out and repeat behind.

21

Outside-reverse-fold.

22

Crimp-fold.

23

Reverse-fold the head.

24

Stick Horse

Pop-Up Horse Card

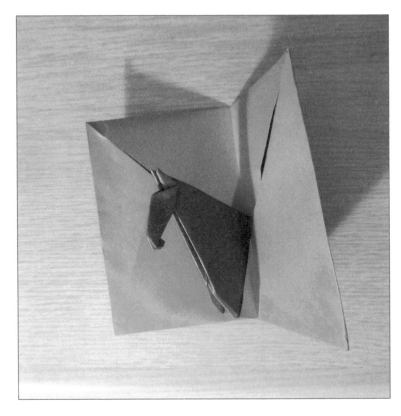

Designed by Sy Chen
Taiwan/USA
Originally diagrammed by Sy Chen

Surprise someone with a greeting card
that says "Neigh!"

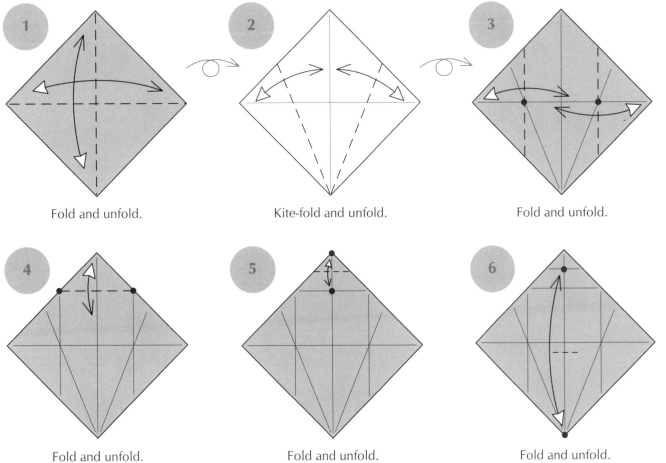

1 Fold and unfold.

2 Kite-fold and unfold.

3 Fold and unfold.

4 Fold and unfold.

5 Fold and unfold.

6 Fold and unfold.

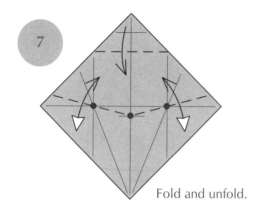

7

Fold and unfold.

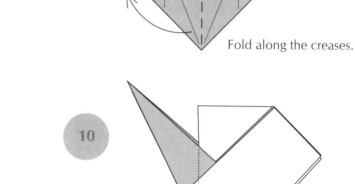

8

Fold along the creases.

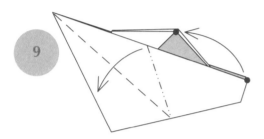

9

Squash-fold so the dots meet. Repeat behind.

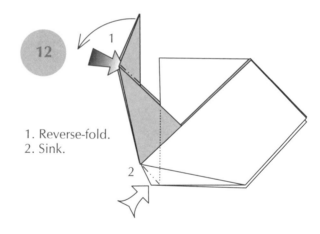

10

Fold and unfold so the dot lines up with the hidden edge.

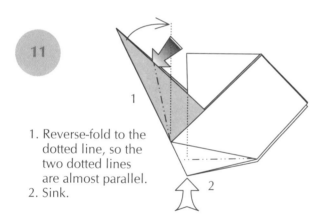

11

1. Reverse-fold to the dotted line, so the two dotted lines are almost parallel.
2. Sink.

12

1. Reverse-fold.
2. Sink.

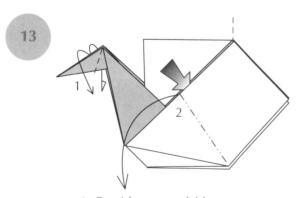

13

1. Outside-reverse-fold.
2. Squash-fold and repeat behind.

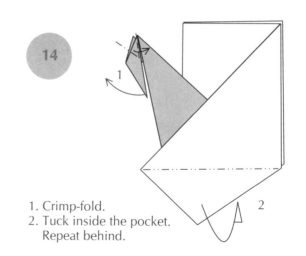

14

1. Crimp-fold.
2. Tuck inside the pocket. Repeat behind.

15

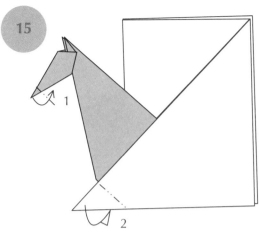

1. Reverse-fold.
2. Tuck inside the pocket.
   Repeat behind.

16

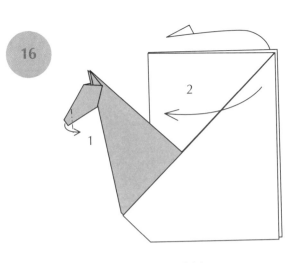

1. Reverse-fold.
2. Spread the card.

17

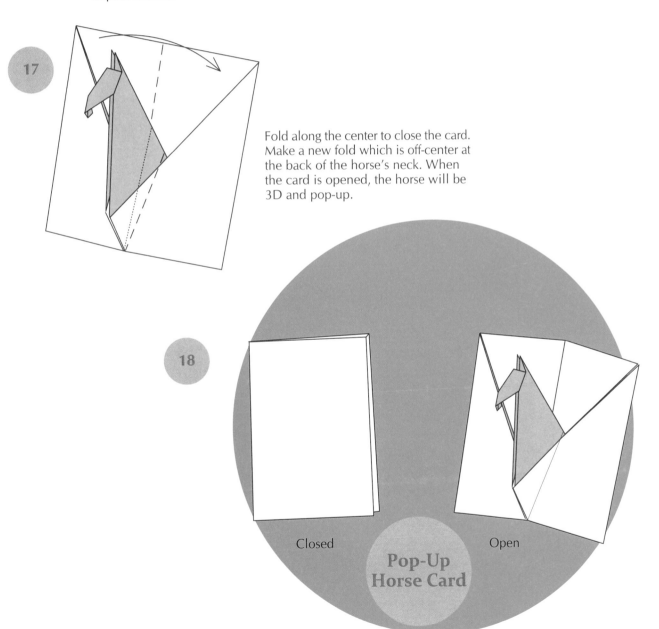

Fold along the center to close the card.
Make a new fold which is off-center at
the back of the horse's neck. When
the card is opened, the horse will be
3D and pop-up.

18

Closed

Open

**Pop-Up
Horse Card**

Rocking Horse

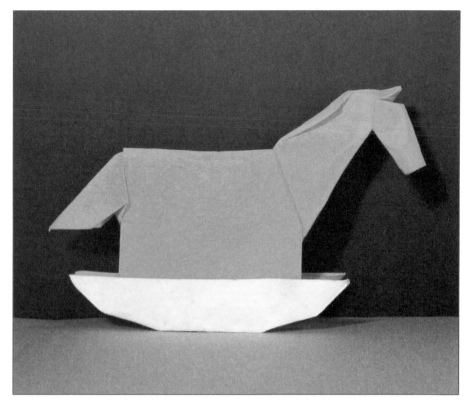

Designed by John Montroll

The history of the rocking horse goes back to ancient civilizations of Greece and Egypt. Beginning with wheels on the feet of the toy horse, the modern rocking horse evolved during the Industrial Revolution in England, and the wealthy would let their children practice horseback riding on rocking horses before trying to ride a real horse.

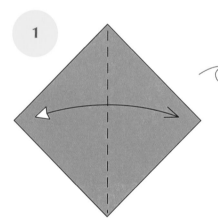

1

Fold and unfold.

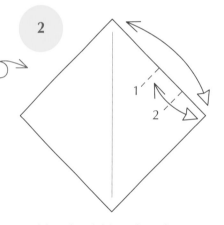

2

Fold and unfold on the edge twice to find the quarter mark.

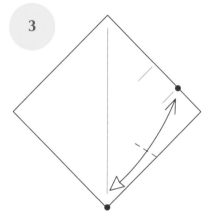

3

Fold and unfold on the edge.

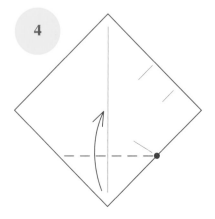

4

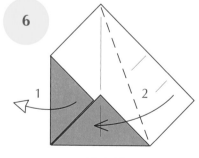

5

6

1. Unfold.
2. Valley-fold.

7

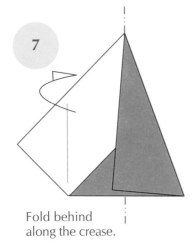

Fold behind along the crease.

8

Bring the dot to the line.

9

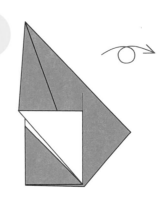

10

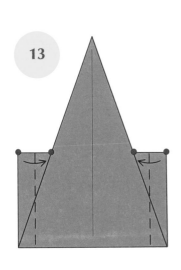

11

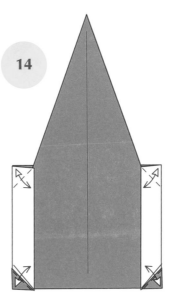

12

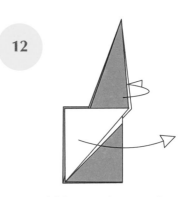

Unfold. Some layers will overlap on the upper part.

13

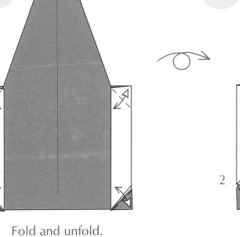

14

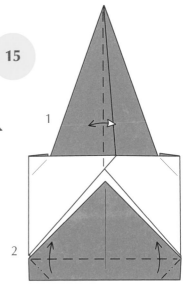

Fold and unfold.

15

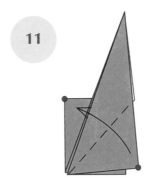

1
2

1. Fold and unfold along the center crease.
2. Petal-fold.

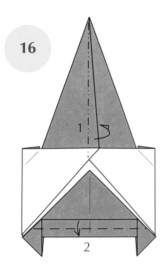

16

1. Mountain-fold.
2. Fold a thin strip.

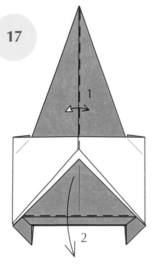

17

1. Repeat steps 15–16 on the right.
2. Fold down.

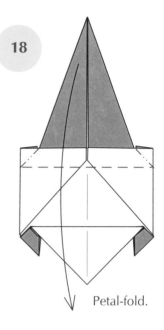

18

Petal-fold.

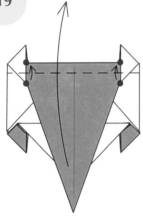

19

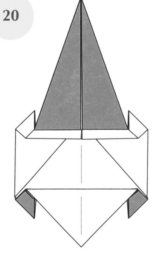

20

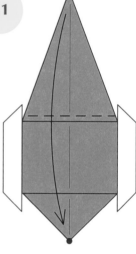

21

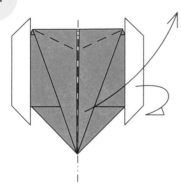

22

Fold the neck up while folding in half. Rotate.

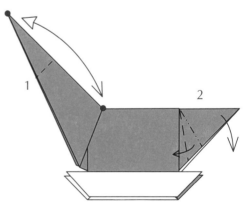

23

1. Fold and unfold.
2. Crimp-fold.

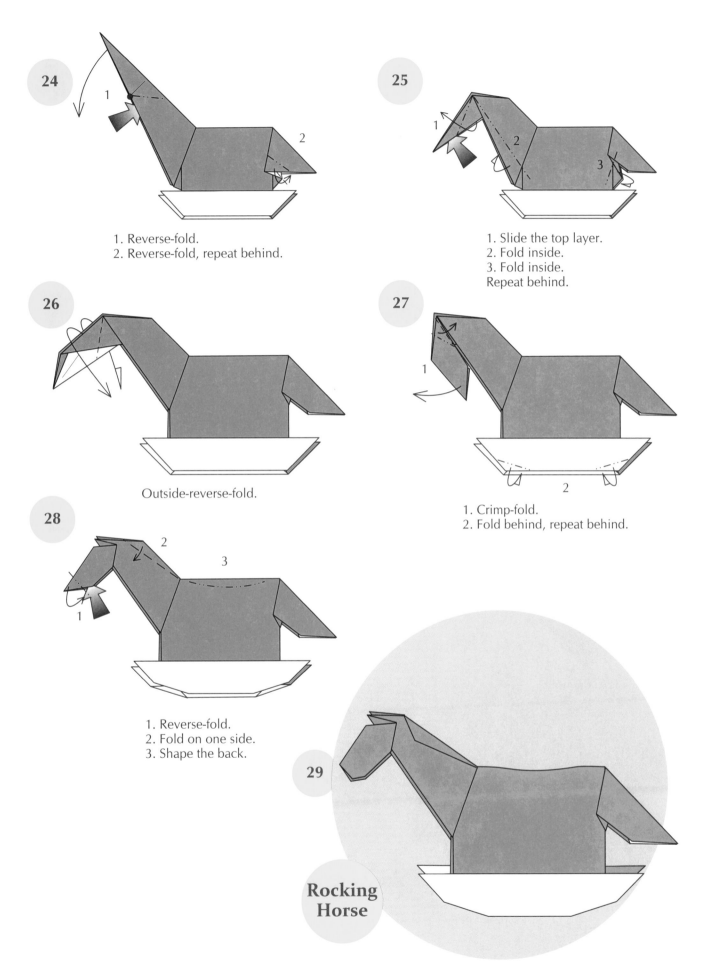

24

1. Reverse-fold.
2. Reverse-fold, repeat behind.

25

1. Slide the top layer.
2. Fold inside.
3. Fold inside.
Repeat behind.

26

Outside-reverse-fold.

27

1. Crimp-fold.
2. Fold behind, repeat behind.

28

1. Reverse-fold.
2. Fold on one side.
3. Shape the back.

29

Rocking Horse

Colorful Horse & Bookmark

Designed by Evi Binzinger
Germany

http://www.kunstkauz.de/impressum.htm

These models highlight stunning color patterns on both sides.

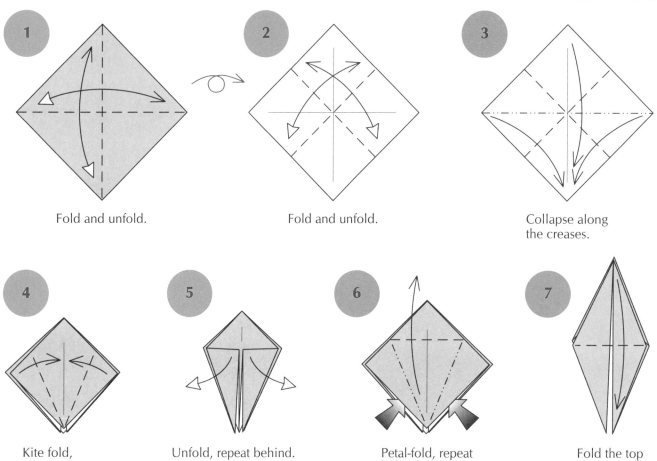

1

Fold and unfold.

2

Fold and unfold.

3

Collapse along the creases.

4

Kite fold, repeat behind.

5

Unfold, repeat behind.

6

Petal-fold, repeat behind.

7

Fold the top layer down.

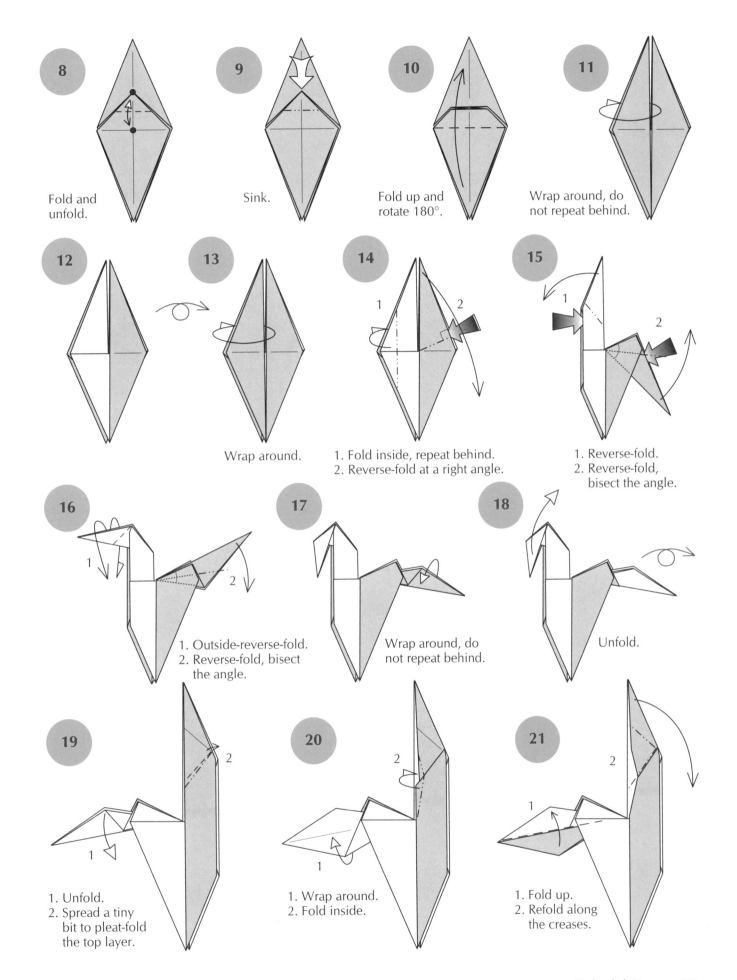

8 Fold and unfold.

9 Sink.

10 Fold up and rotate 180°.

11 Wrap around, do not repeat behind.

12

13 Wrap around.

14
1. Fold inside, repeat behind.
2. Reverse-fold at a right angle.

15
1. Reverse-fold.
2. Reverse-fold, bisect the angle.

16
1. Outside-reverse-fold.
2. Reverse-fold, bisect the angle.

17 Wrap around, do not repeat behind.

18 Unfold.

19
1. Unfold.
2. Spread a tiny bit to pleat-fold the top layer.

20
1. Wrap around.
2. Fold inside.

21
1. Fold up.
2. Refold along the creases.

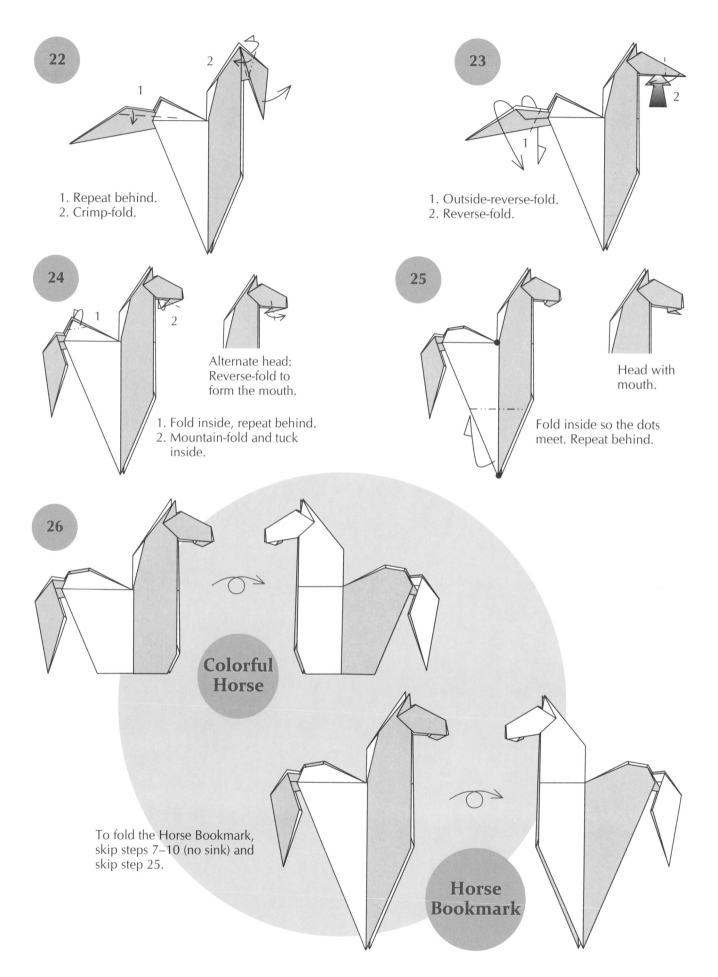

22

1. Repeat behind.
2. Crimp-fold.

23

1. Outside-reverse-fold.
2. Reverse-fold.

24

Alternate head:
Reverse-fold to
form the mouth.

1. Fold inside, repeat behind.
2. Mountain-fold and tuck
   inside.

25

Head with
mouth.

Fold inside so the dots
meet. Repeat behind.

26

**Colorful
Horse**

**Horse
Bookmark**

To fold the Horse Bookmark,
skip steps 7–10 (no sink) and
skip step 25.

General

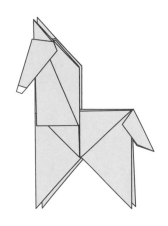

The models in this section capture the uniqueness of the horse as expressed by various origami artists.

Simple Pony

Designed by John Montroll

This simple pony is a good model for the new folder. The head details are similar to those of several horses.

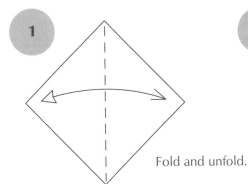

1 Fold and unfold.

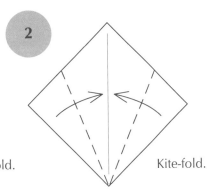

2 Kite-fold.

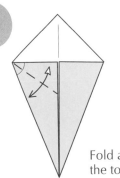

3 Fold and unfold the top layer.

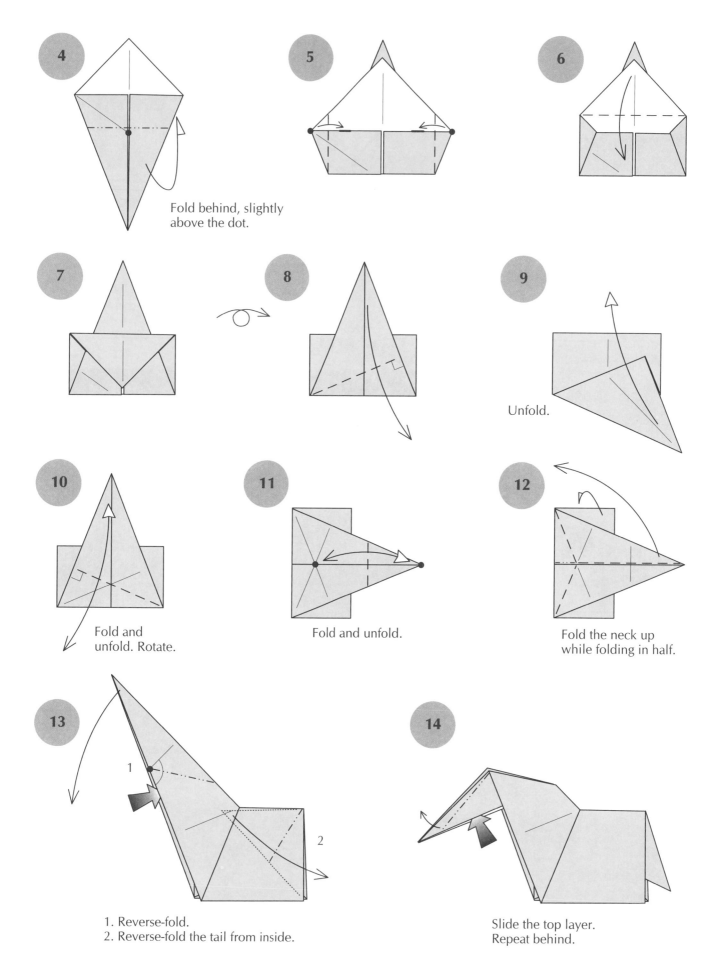

4

Fold behind, slightly above the dot.

5

6

7

8

9

Unfold.

10

Fold and unfold. Rotate.

11

Fold and unfold.

12

Fold the neck up while folding in half.

13

1. Reverse-fold.
2. Reverse-fold the tail from inside.

14

Slide the top layer. Repeat behind.

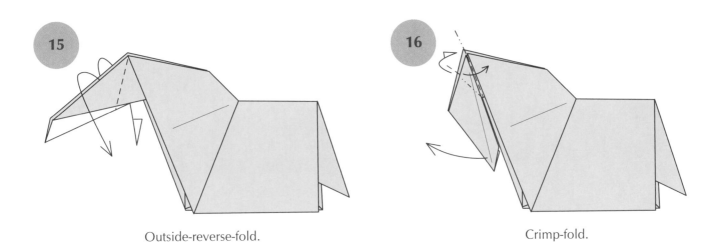

15 Outside-reverse-fold.

16 Crimp-fold.

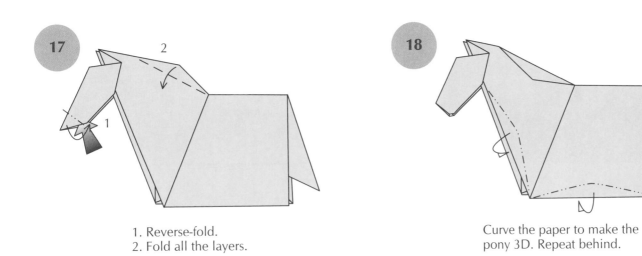

17
1. Reverse-fold.
2. Fold all the layers.

18 Curve the paper to make the pony 3D. Repeat behind.

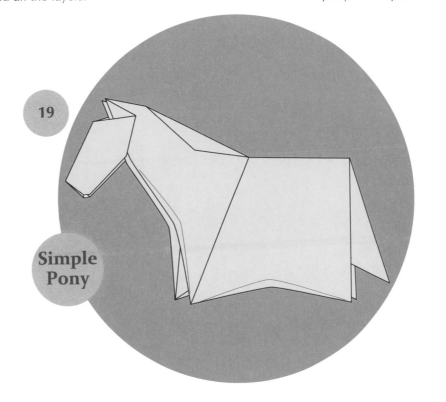

19 Simple Pony

Classic Horse

Designed by John Montroll

This horse is fold from the Dog Base, step 27. I deveoped this base some time ago. It brought a new level of structure and propotion, to form nonspreading models with detail, yet with some simplicity. This structure allows for many variations, one example is with Robert J. Lang's Horse (page 54).

1

Fold in half.

2

Fold and unfold the top layer. Repeat behind.

3

Fold and unfold.

4

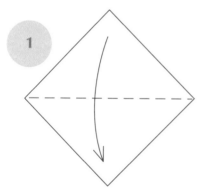

Reverse-fold.

5

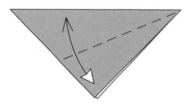

Squash-fold along the crease. Repeat behind.

6

Repeat behind.

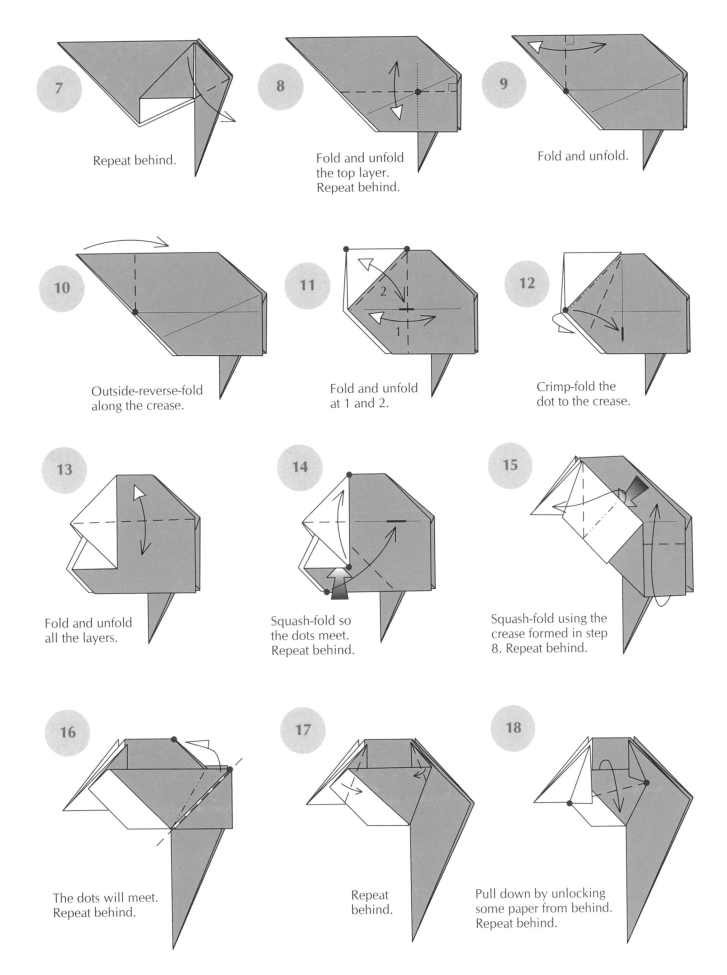

7

Repeat behind.

8

Fold and unfold
the top layer.
Repeat behind.

9

Fold and unfold.

10

Outside-reverse-fold
along the crease.

11

Fold and unfold
at 1 and 2.

12

Crimp-fold the
dot to the crease.

13

Fold and unfold
all the layers.

14

Squash-fold so
the dots meet.
Repeat behind.

15

Squash-fold using the
crease formed in step
8. Repeat behind.

16

The dots will meet.
Repeat behind.

17

Repeat
behind.

18

Pull down by unlocking
some paper from behind.
Repeat behind.

Classic Horse 31

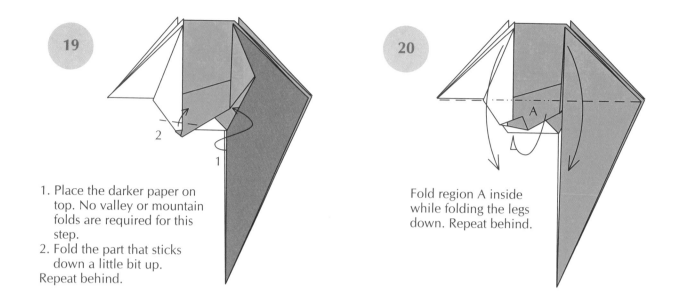

19

1. Place the darker paper on top. No valley or mountain folds are required for this step.
2. Fold the part that sticks down a little bit up. Repeat behind.

20

Fold region A inside while folding the legs down. Repeat behind.

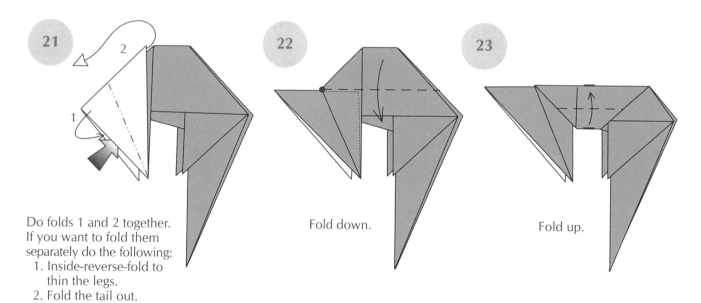

21

Do folds 1 and 2 together. If you want to fold them separately do the following:
1. Inside-reverse-fold to thin the legs.
2. Fold the tail out.

22

Fold down.

23

Fold up.

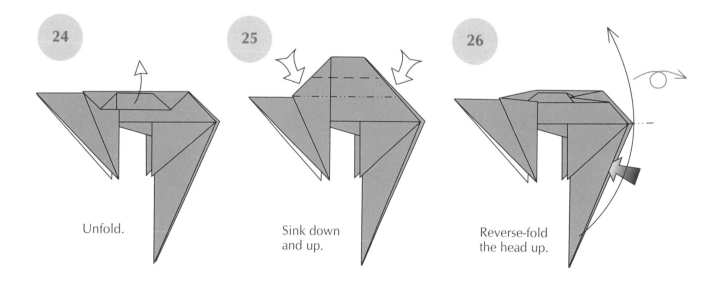

24

Unfold.

25

Sink down and up.

26

Reverse-fold the head up.

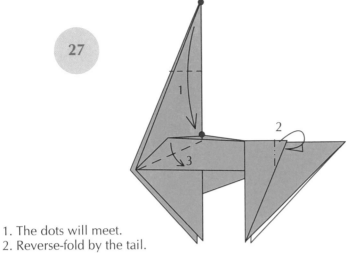

27

1. The dots will meet.
2. Reverse-fold by the tail.
3. Repeat behind.

28

1. Squash-fold so the dot meets the edge.
2. Fold behind by the dots.

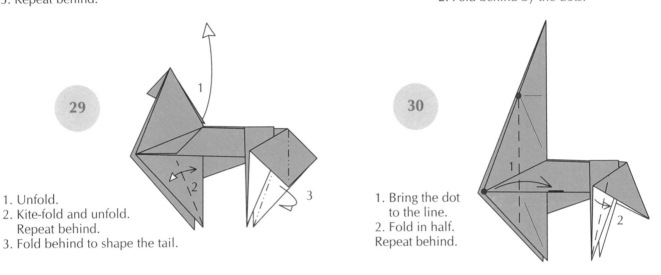

29

1. Unfold.
2. Kite-fold and unfold. Repeat behind.
3. Fold behind to shape the tail.

30

1. Bring the dot to the line.
2. Fold in half. Repeat behind.

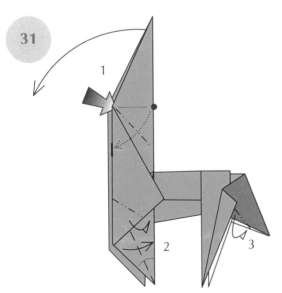

31

1. Reverse-fold so the dot meets the edge.
2. Fold the leg in half.
3. Form the tail. Note that the darker region will be on the top after this fold. Repeat behind.

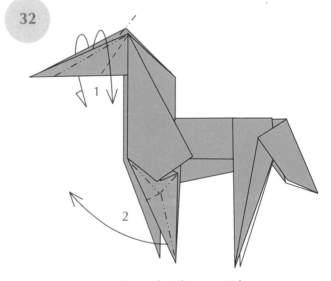

32

1. Spread with an outside reverse fold to form the head.
2. Double-rabbit-ear the front legs, repeat behind.

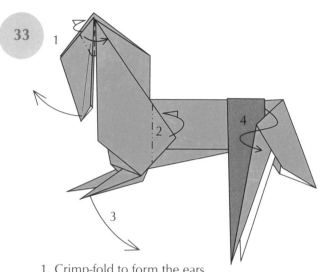

33

1. Crimp-fold to form the ears and fold the head up a bit.
2. Fold behind, repeat behind.
3. Slide only one leg down.
4. Place the darker region above. Repeat behind.

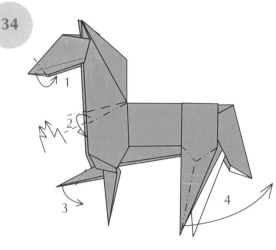

34

1. Reverse-fold.
2. Crimp-fold to bend the neck.
3. Reverse-fold the front leg.
4. Double-rabbit-ear the hind leg. Repeat behind.

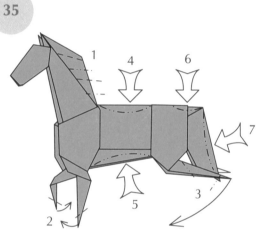

35

1. Pleat the mane.
2. Form the front hooves.
3. Shape the hind legs and hooves.
4. Make the back 3D.
5. Make the underside 3D.
6. Shape the top of the tail.
7. Shape the tail.

36

Classic Horse

Foal

Designed by John Montroll

A foal is a young horse up to one year old. The male foal is a colt, the female is a filly. Within an hour of birth, the foal can stand; within hours it can trot and canter and by the next day it can gallop. After a year, the horse is a yearling. A foal is not ready to be ridden or used for work.

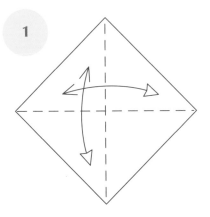

1

Fold and unfold.

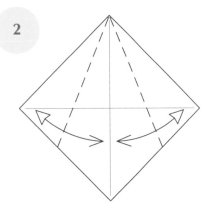

2

Kite-fold and unfold.

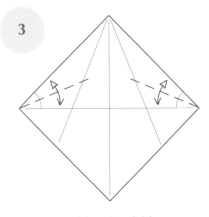

3

Fold and unfold.

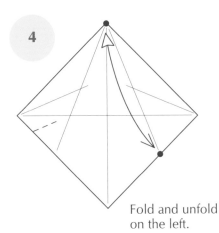

4

Fold and unfold on the left.

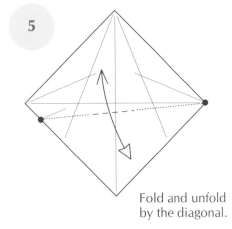

5

Fold and unfold by the diagonal.

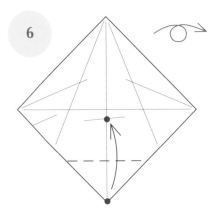

6

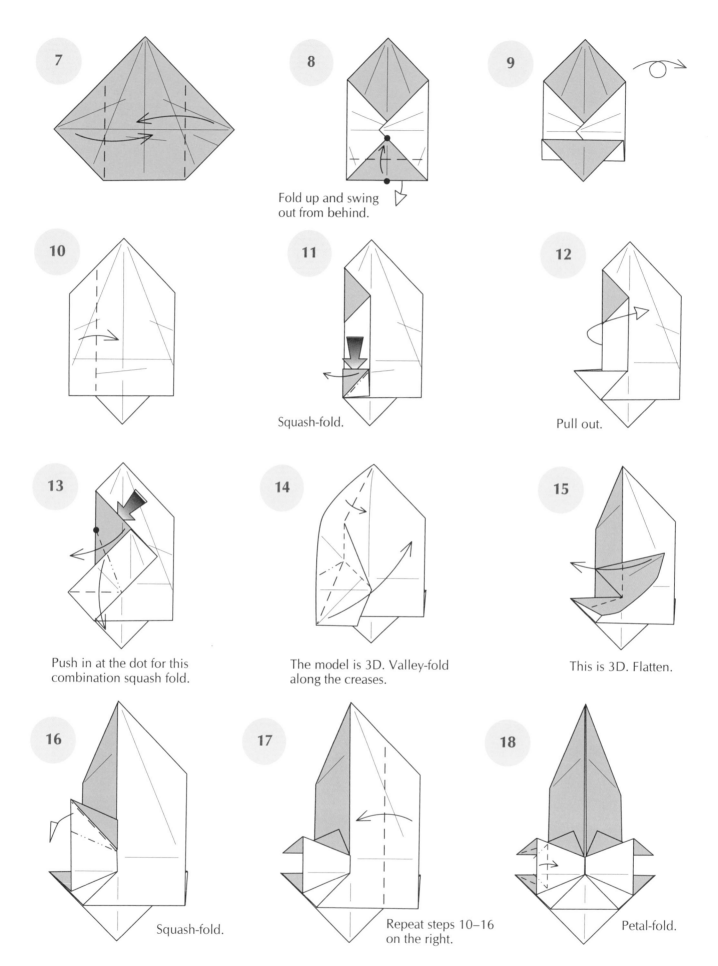

7

8

Fold up and swing
out from behind.

9

10

11

Squash-fold.

12

Pull out.

13

Push in at the dot for this
combination squash fold.

14

The model is 3D. Valley-fold
along the creases.

15

This is 3D. Flatten.

16

Squash-fold.

17

Repeat steps 10–16
on the right.

18

Petal-fold.

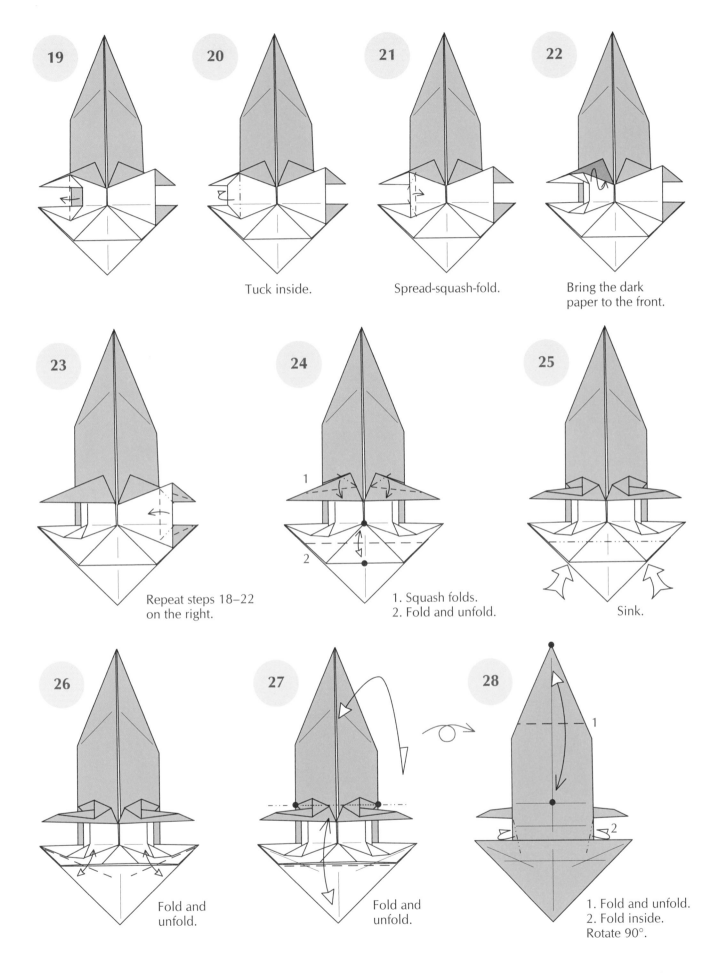

19

20

Tuck inside.

21

Spread-squash-fold.

22

Bring the dark
paper to the front.

23

Repeat steps 18–22
on the right.

24

1. Squash folds.
2. Fold and unfold.

25

Sink.

26

Fold and
unfold.

27

Fold and
unfold.

28

1. Fold and unfold.
2. Fold inside.
Rotate 90°.

Foal 37

29

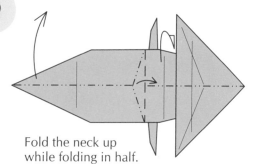

Fold the neck up
while folding in half.

30

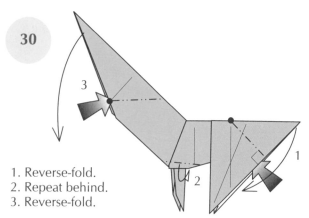

1. Reverse-fold.
2. Repeat behind.
3. Reverse-fold.

31

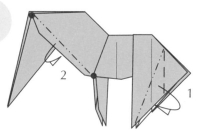

1. This is similar to a reverse-fold.
2. Fold inside.
Repeat behind.

32

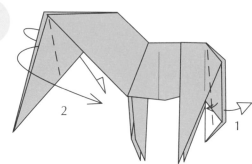

1. Repeat behind to shape the tail.
2. Outside-reverse-fold.

33

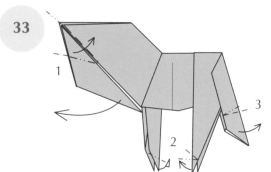

1. Crimp-fold.
2. Spread, repeat behind.
3. Crimp-fold.

34

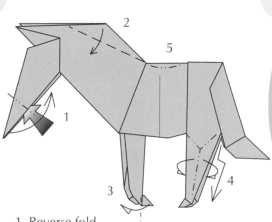

1. Reverse-fold.
2. Fold all the layers.
3. Repeat behind.
4. Shape the legs, repeat behind.
5. Shape the back.

35

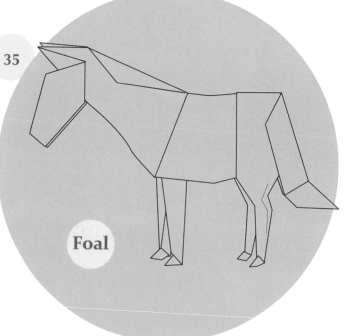

Foal

Dollar Bill Horse

Designed by John Montroll

Dollar bill folding is very popular. This horse design uses ideas from the Dog Base, see the Classic Horse (page 30).

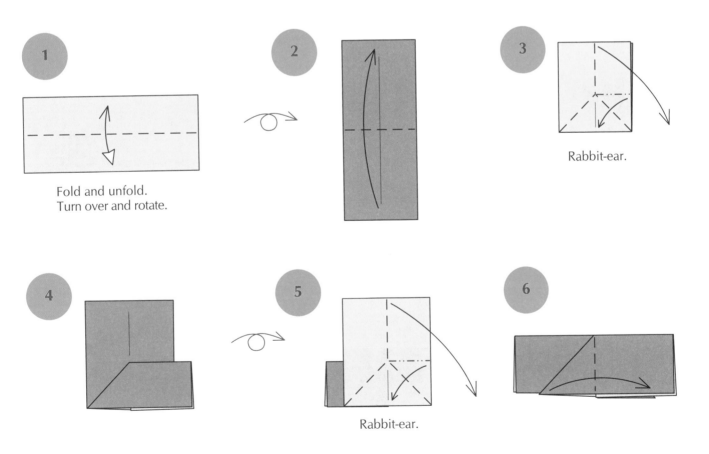

1

Fold and unfold.
Turn over and rotate.

2

3

Rabbit-ear.

4

5

Rabbit-ear.

6

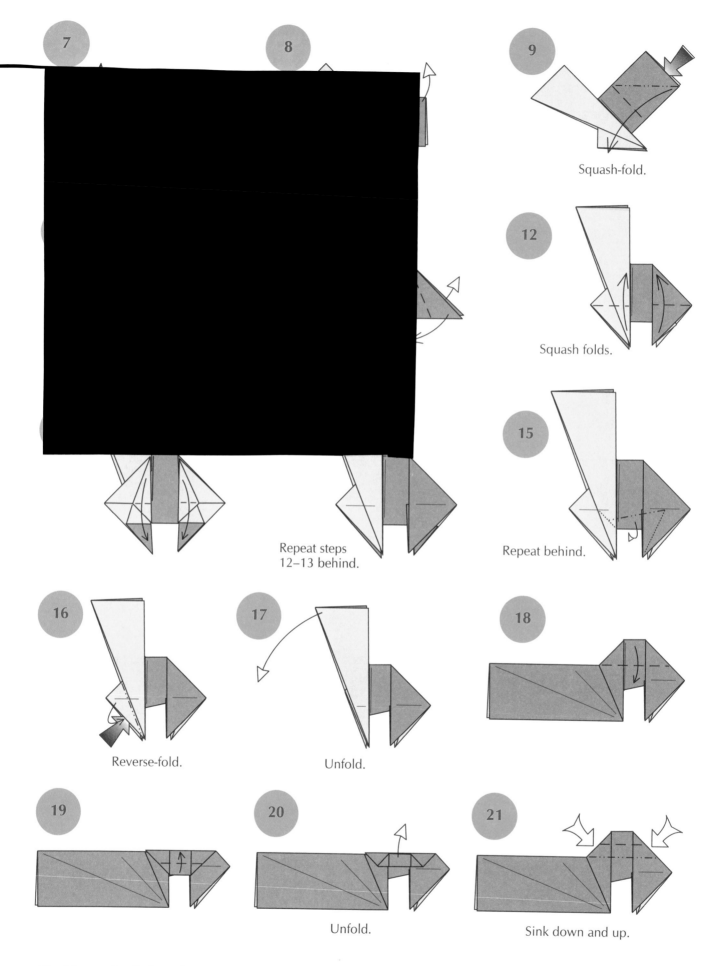

7

8

9

Squash-fold.

12

Squash folds.

15

Repeat steps
12–13 behind.

Repeat behind.

16

Reverse-fold.

17

Unfold.

18

19

20

Unfold.

21

Sink down and up.

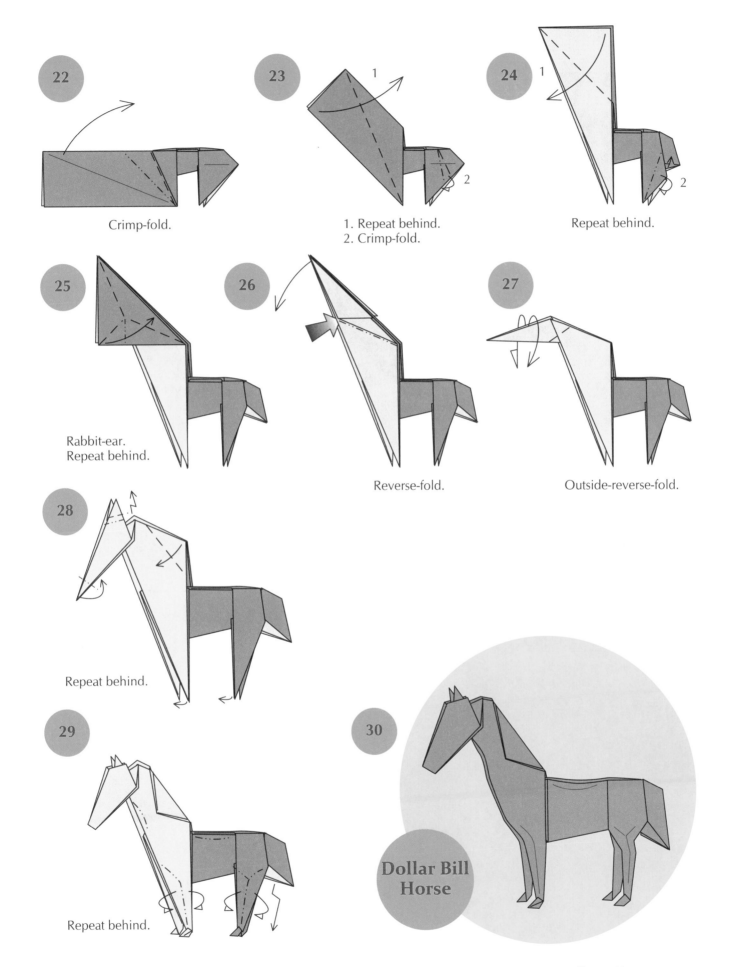

22 Crimp-fold.

23
1. Repeat behind.
2. Crimp-fold.

24 Repeat behind.

25 Rabbit-ear.
Repeat behind.

26 Reverse-fold.

27 Outside-reverse-fold.

28 Repeat behind.

29 Repeat behind.

30 Dollar Bill Horse

Dollar Bill Horse 41

Horseback Riding

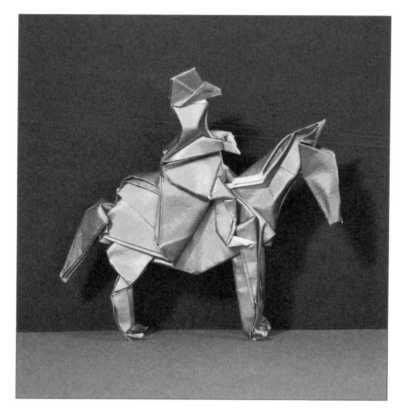

Designed by John Montroll

In the early days of humans owning horses, the domesticated horse was not used for riding. It took people a long time to invent the equipment to use for that purpose and to figure out how to train the horse, who naturally would not allow it.

1

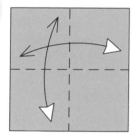

Fold and unfold.

2

Blintz fold: Fold the four corners to the center.

3

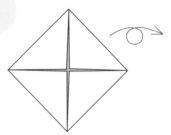

4

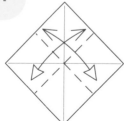

Fold and unfold.

5

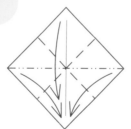

This is similar to the Preliminary Fold.

6

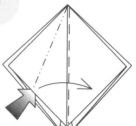

(Diagram enlarged.) Squash-fold.

7

Petal-fold.

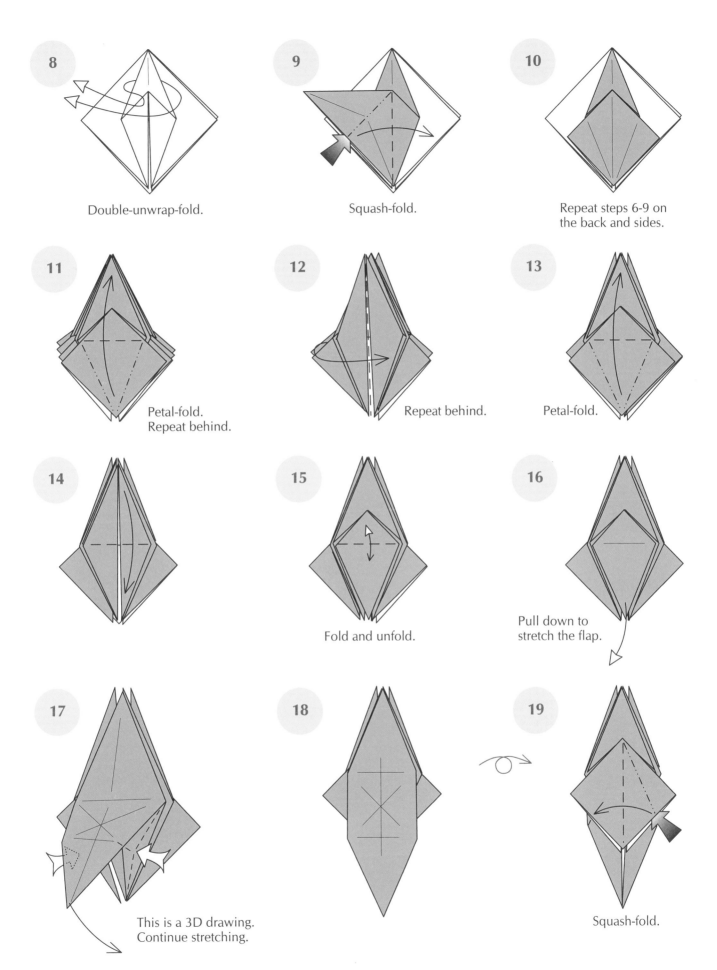

8 Double-unwrap-fold.

9 Squash-fold.

10 Repeat steps 6-9 on the back and sides.

11 Petal-fold. Repeat behind.

12 Repeat behind.

13 Petal-fold.

14

15 Fold and unfold.

16 Pull down to stretch the flap.

17 This is a 3D drawing. Continue stretching.

18

19 Squash-fold.

Horseback Riding 43

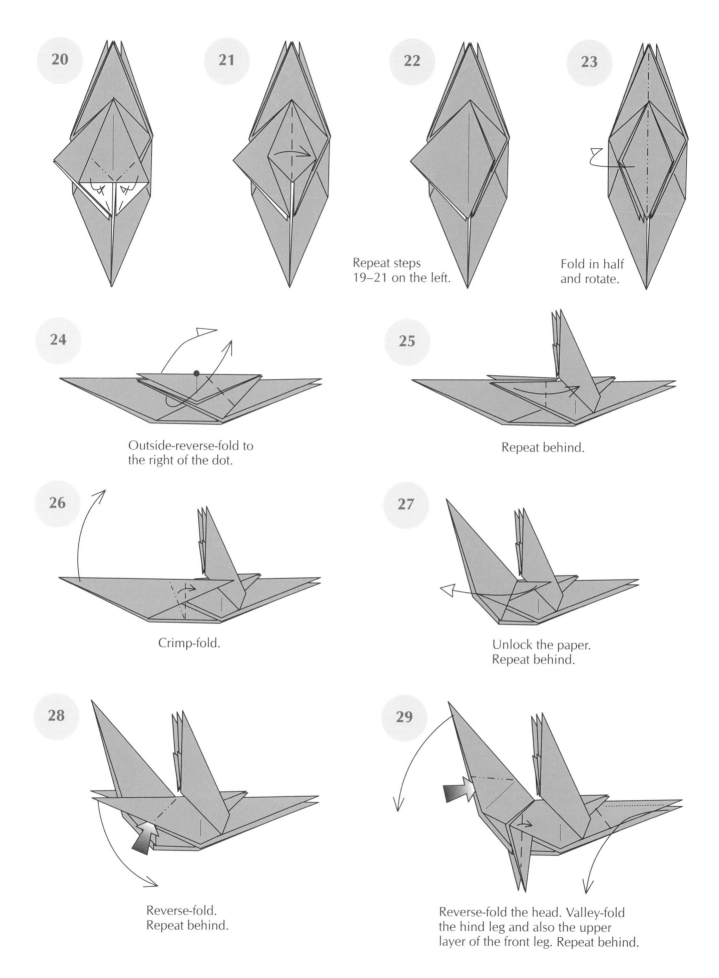

20

21

22

Repeat steps
19–21 on the left.

23

Fold in half
and rotate.

24

Outside-reverse-fold to
the right of the dot.

25

Repeat behind.

26

Crimp-fold.

27

Unlock the paper.
Repeat behind.

28

Reverse-fold.
Repeat behind.

29

Reverse-fold the head. Valley-fold
the hind leg and also the upper
layer of the front leg. Repeat behind.

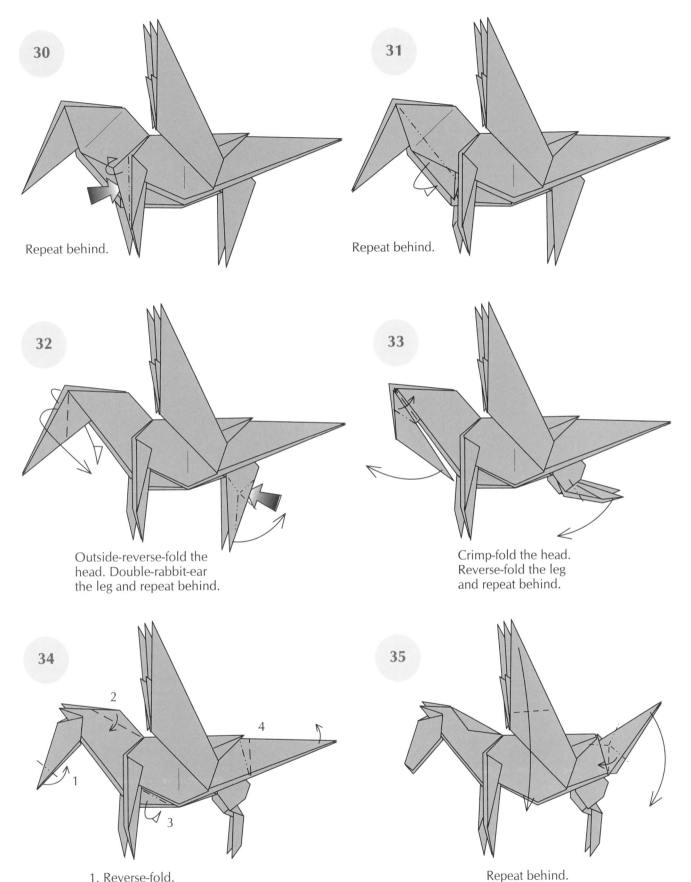

30

Repeat behind.

31

Repeat behind.

32

Outside-reverse-fold the
head. Double-rabbit-ear
the leg and repeat behind.

33

Crimp-fold the head.
Reverse-fold the leg
and repeat behind.

34

1. Reverse-fold.
2. Fold down on one side.
3. Repeat behind.
4. Crimp-fold.

35

Repeat behind.

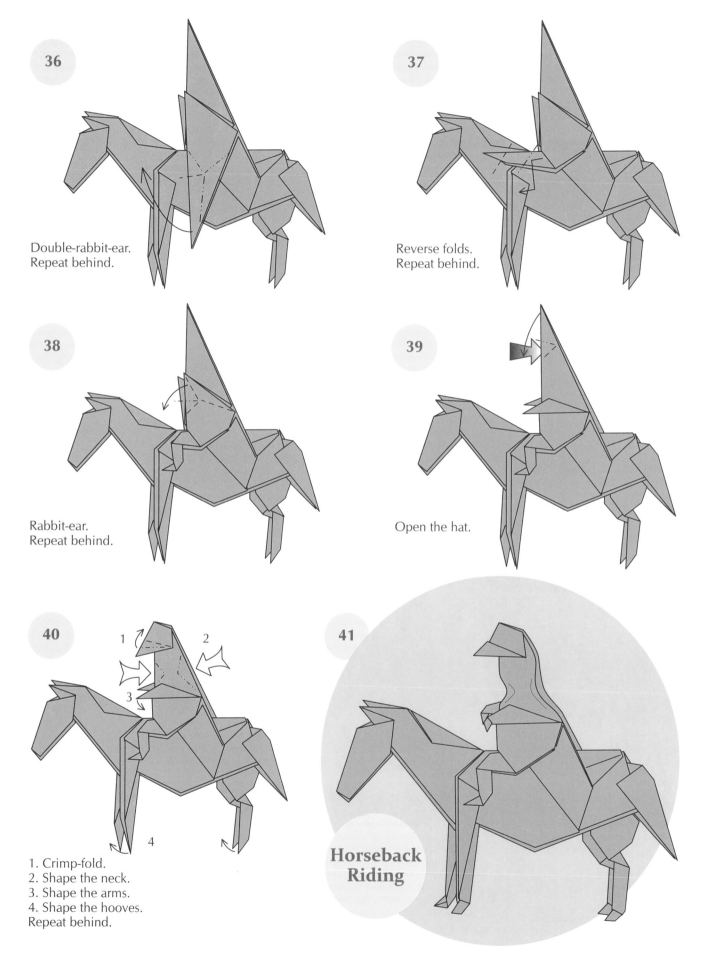

36

Double-rabbit-ear.
Repeat behind.

37

Reverse folds.
Repeat behind.

38

Rabbit-ear.
Repeat behind.

39

Open the hat.

40

1
2
3
4

1. Crimp-fold.
2. Shape the neck.
3. Shape the arms.
4. Shape the hooves.
Repeat behind.

41

**Horseback
Riding**

Ponytail Pony

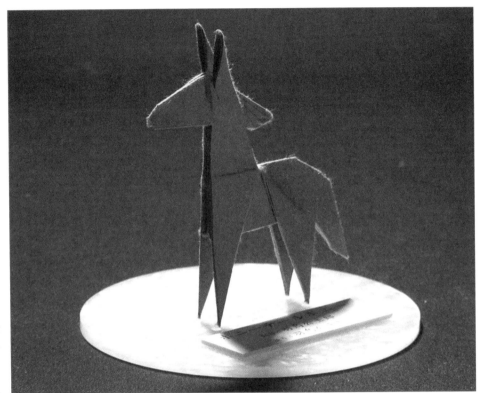

Designed by Koshiro Hatori
Japan

http://origami.ousaan.com/

Ponies are small horses. They have been used as working animals, often for freight transport. They are intelligent and friendly, and children can ride on them.

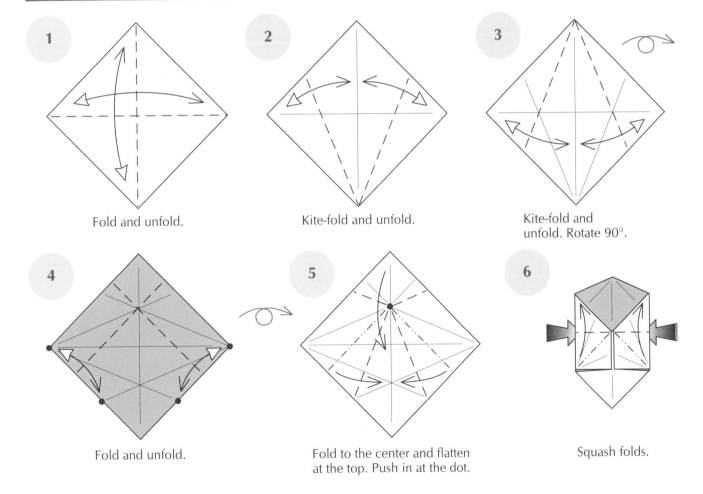

1 Fold and unfold.

2 Kite-fold and unfold.

3 Kite-fold and unfold. Rotate 90°.

4 Fold and unfold.

5 Fold to the center and flatten at the top. Push in at the dot.

6 Squash folds.

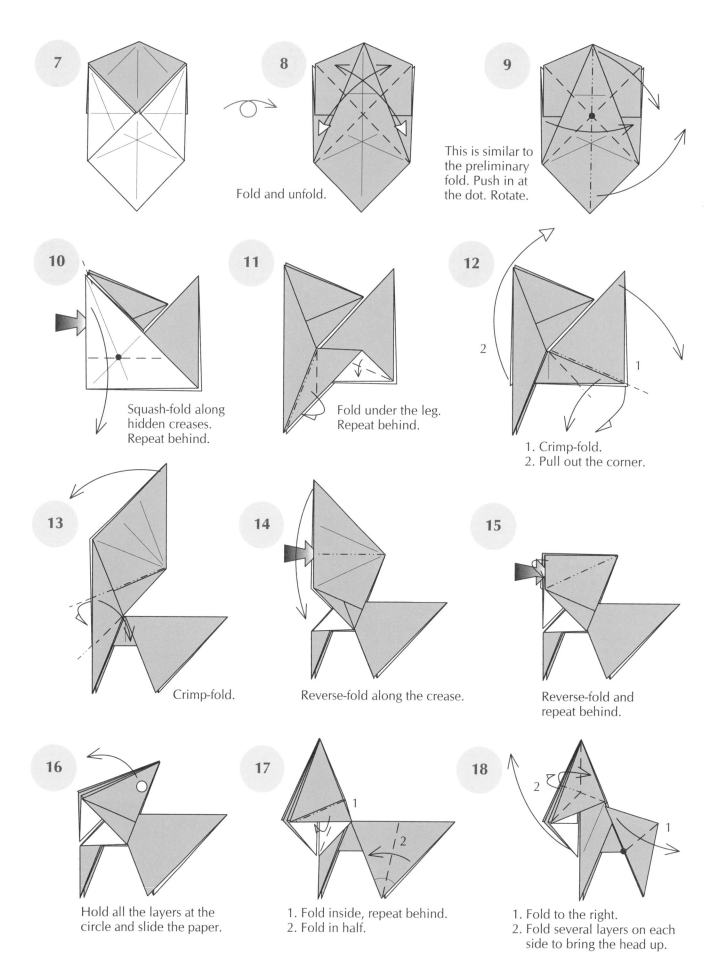

7

8 Fold and unfold.

9 This is similar to the preliminary fold. Push in at the dot. Rotate.

10 Squash-fold along hidden creases. Repeat behind.

11 Fold under the leg. Repeat behind.

12
1. Crimp-fold.
2. Pull out the corner.

13 Crimp-fold.

14 Reverse-fold along the crease.

15 Reverse-fold and repeat behind.

16 Hold all the layers at the circle and slide the paper.

17
1. Fold inside, repeat behind.
2. Fold in half.

18
1. Fold to the right.
2. Fold several layers on each side to bring the head up.

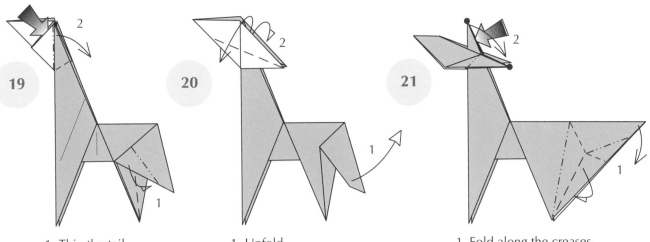

19

1. Thin the tail.
2. Squash-fold, repeat behind.

20

1. Unfold.
2. Outside-reverse-fold.

21

1. Fold along the creases to form the tail. Repeat behind at the same time.
2. Reverse-fold.

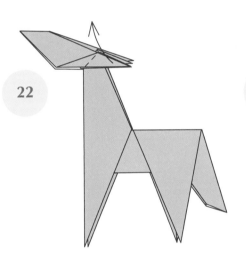

22

Repeat behind.

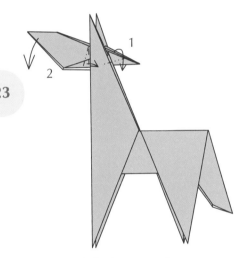

23

1. Slide down two layers, repeat behind.
2. Crimp-fold.

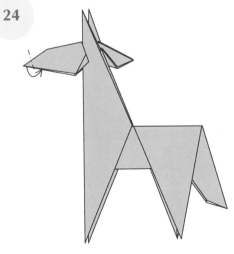

24

Reverse-fold.

25

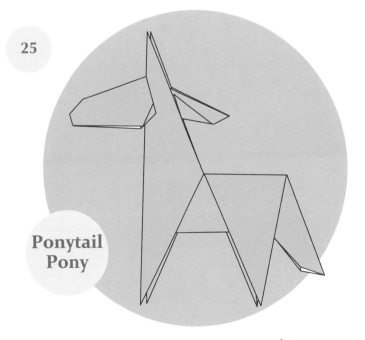

Ponytail Pony

Horse

Designed by Seo Won Seon
South Korea
Originally diagrammed by Seo Won Seon

http://www.flickr.com/photos/origamist/

Horses have keener hearing than people. They can hear lower and higher sounds than humans, and can move their ears to better focus on the sounds. Their sense of smell is also far better than ours. For example, in the desert, horses can smell water from far away.

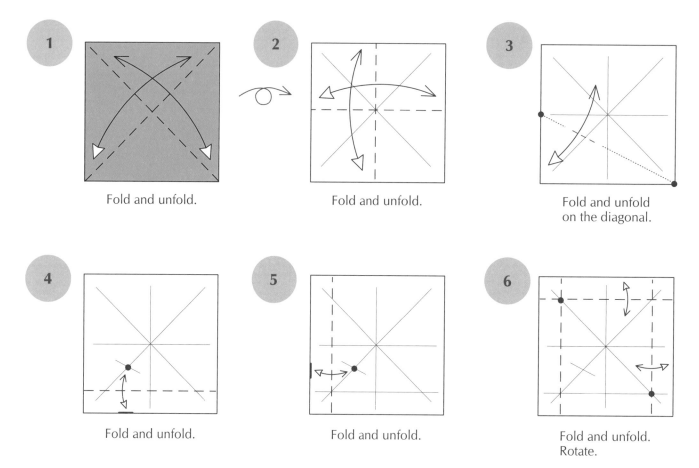

1

Fold and unfold.

2

Fold and unfold.

3

Fold and unfold on the diagonal.

4

Fold and unfold.

5

Fold and unfold.

6

Fold and unfold. Rotate.

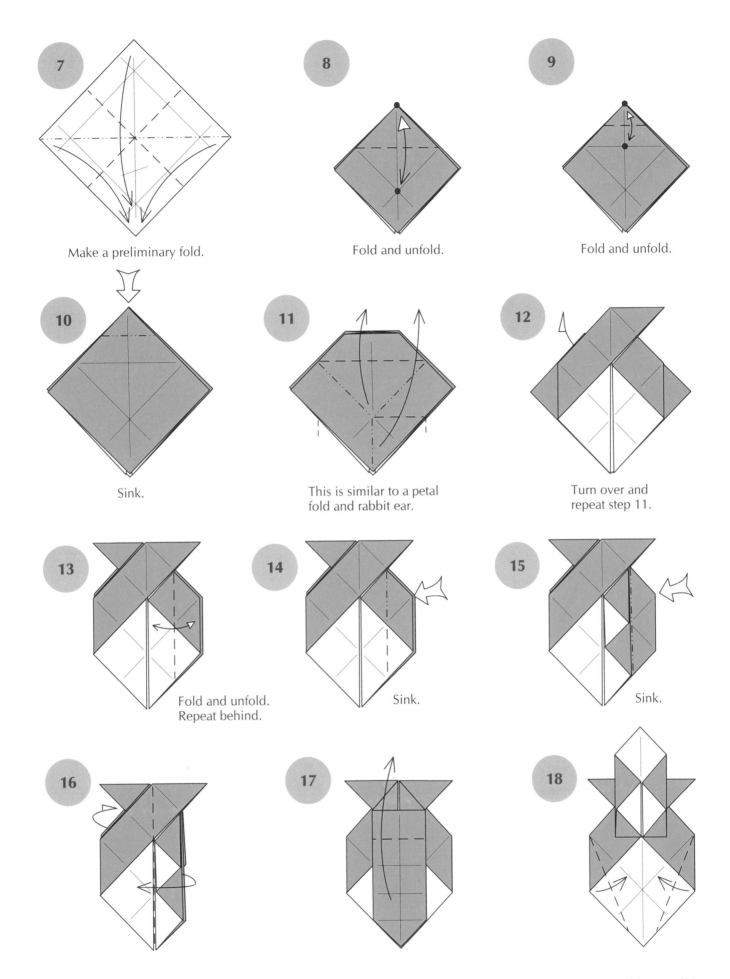

7 Make a preliminary fold.

8 Fold and unfold.

9 Fold and unfold.

10 Sink.

11 This is similar to a petal fold and rabbit ear.

12 Turn over and repeat step 11.

13 Fold and unfold. Repeat behind.

14 Sink.

15 Sink.

16

17

18

Horse 51

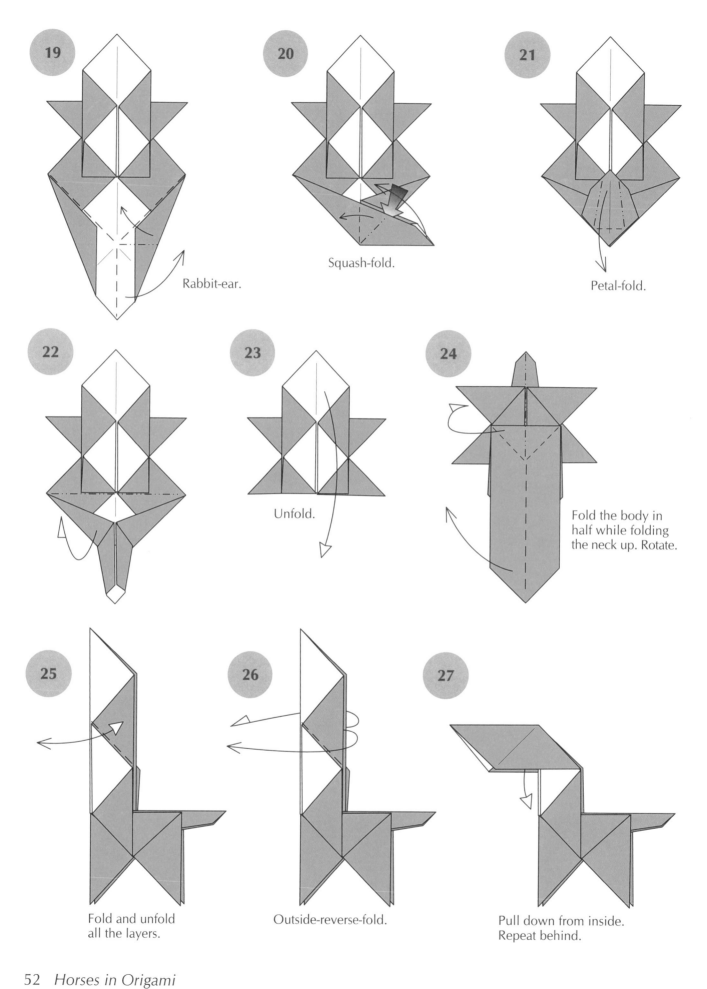

19

Rabbit-ear.

20

Squash-fold.

21

Petal-fold.

22

23

Unfold.

24

Fold the body in half while folding the neck up. Rotate.

25

Fold and unfold all the layers.

26

Outside-reverse-fold.

27

Pull down from inside. Repeat behind.

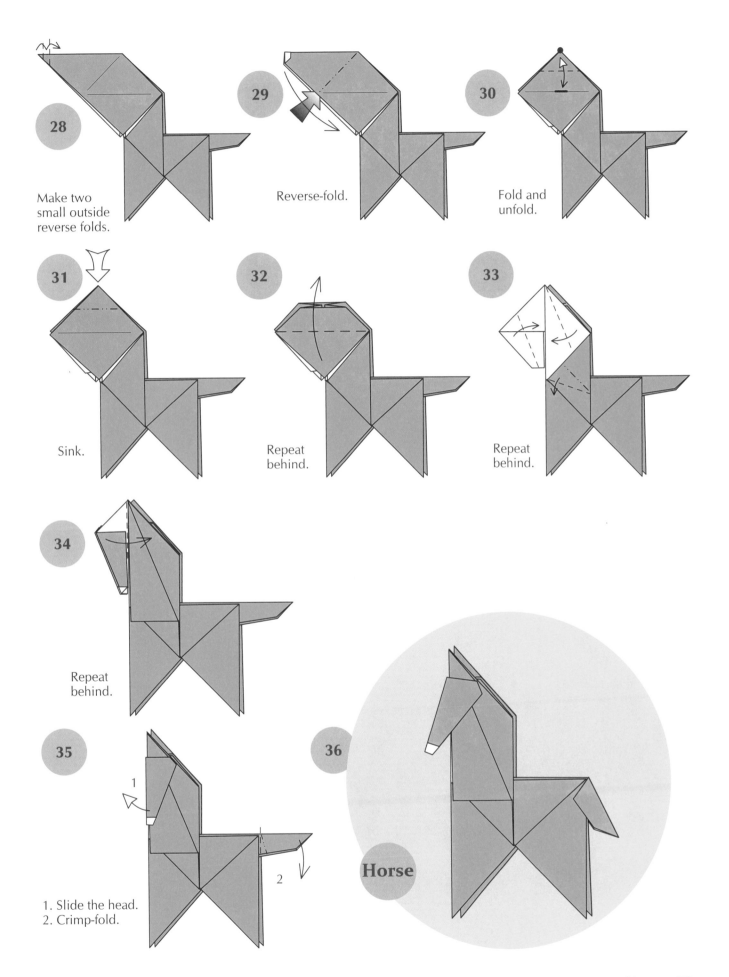

28

Make two small outside reverse folds.

29

Reverse-fold.

30

Fold and unfold.

31

Sink.

32

Repeat behind.

33

Repeat behind.

34

Repeat behind.

35

1. Slide the head.
2. Crimp-fold.

36

Horse

Horse

Designed by Robert J. Lang
USA

http://www.langorigami.com/

Horses are intelligent and have good memories. They communicate through sounds such as whinnying, ear movements, different neck and head positions, and tail swishing. As a prey animal, horses might initially see people as predators, but they can learn to trust and bond with people. Horses are naturally curious and form strong social bonds.

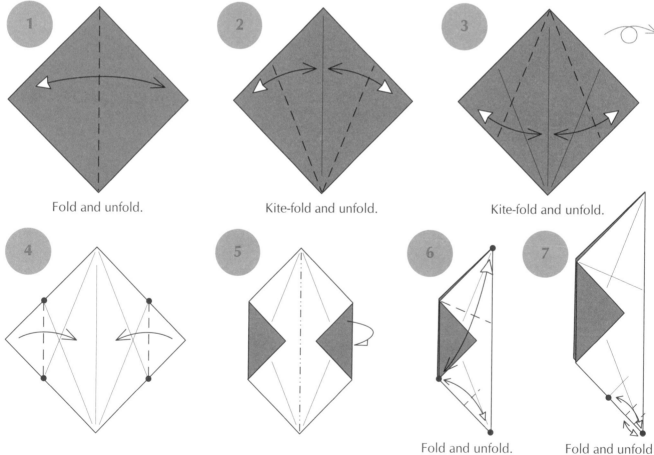

1
Fold and unfold.

2
Kite-fold and unfold.

3
Kite-fold and unfold.

4

5

6
Fold and unfold.

7
Fold and unfold
in half twice.

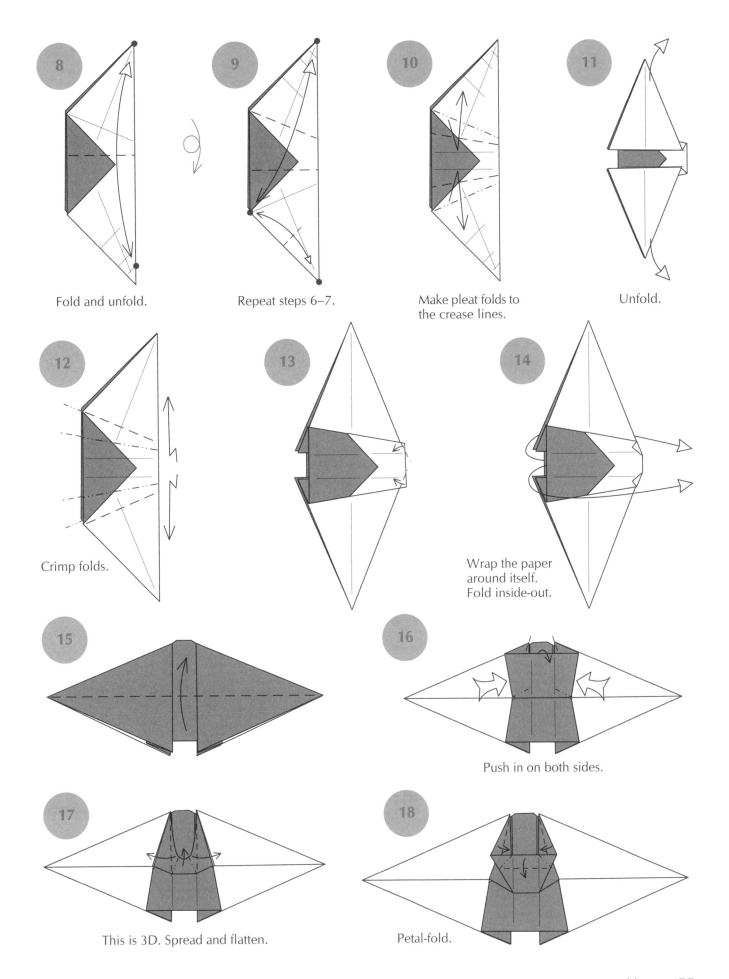

8 Fold and unfold.

9 Repeat steps 6–7.

10 Make pleat folds to the crease lines.

11 Unfold.

12 Crimp folds.

13

14 Wrap the paper around itself. Fold inside-out.

15

16 Push in on both sides.

17 This is 3D. Spread and flatten.

18 Petal-fold.

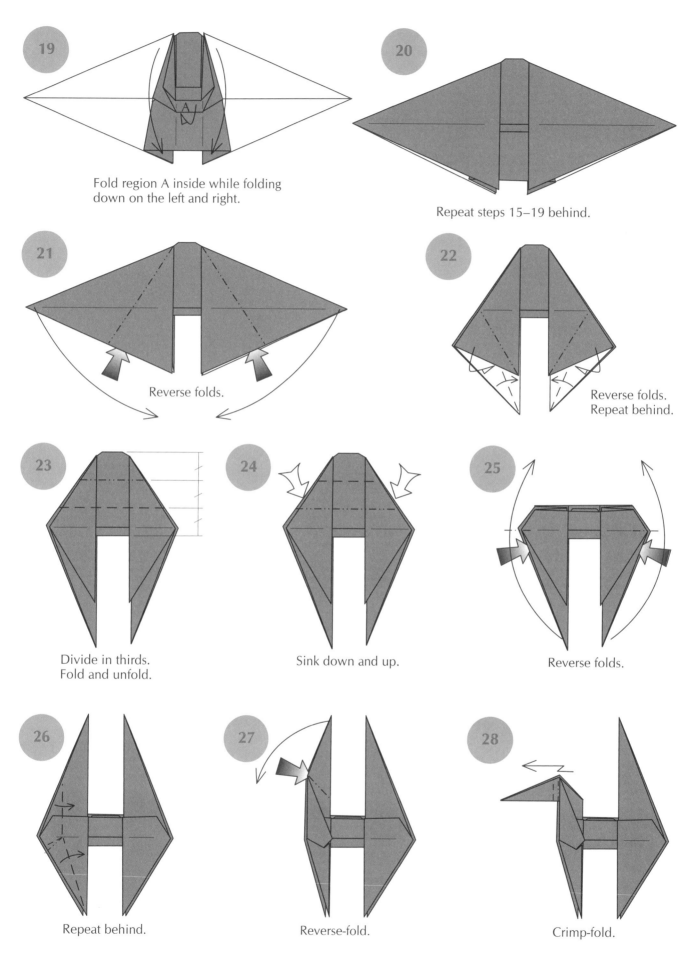

19 Fold region A inside while folding down on the left and right.

20 Repeat steps 15–19 behind.

21 Reverse folds.

22 Reverse folds. Repeat behind.

23 Divide in thirds. Fold and unfold.

24 Sink down and up.

25 Reverse folds.

26 Repeat behind.

27 Reverse-fold.

28 Crimp-fold.

29 Head.

Spread the head.

30

1. Reverse-fold.
2. Repeat behind.

31

Pleat-fold the mane.

32

33

34

1. Fold the top inside.
   Repeat behind.
2. Reverse-fold.

35

1. Shape the legs,
   repeat behind.
2. Pleat-fold the tail.
3. Crimp-fold.

36

Pull out interior layers.
Repeat behind.

37

Horse

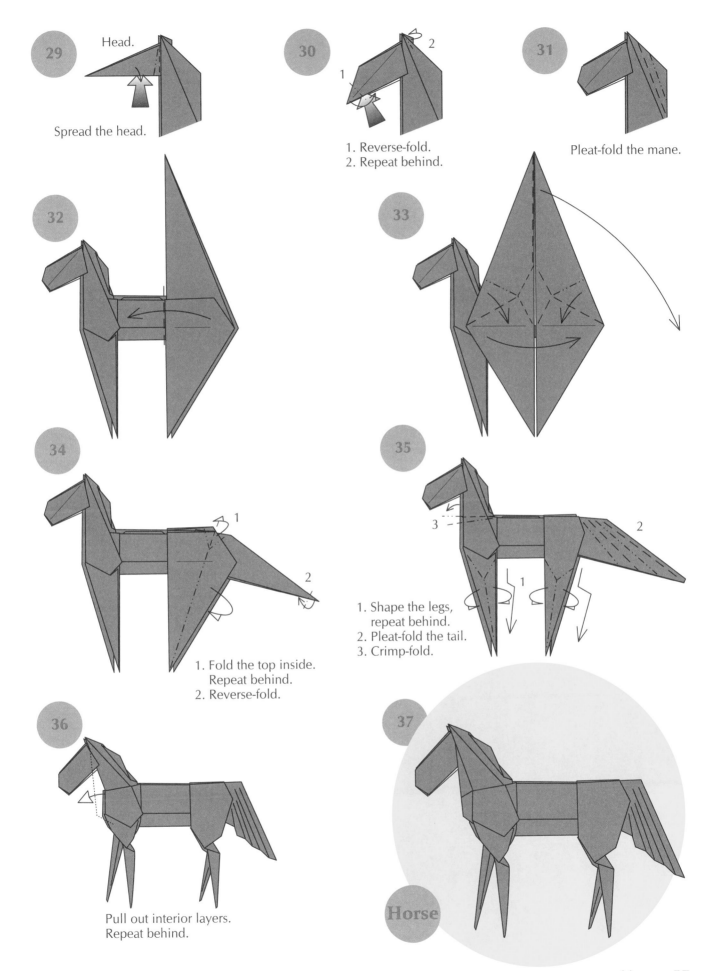

Horse

Designed by Davor Vinko
Croatia

http://www.flickr.com/
photos/davorigami/

Horses move in four natural gaits: walk (4 miles per hour), trot (8 to 12 mph), canter (12 to 15 mph), and gallop (25 to 30 mph). The trot is a two-beat gait. Horses can trot for hours. The cantor is a three-beat gait and the gallop is a four-beat gait. Horses gallop when racing.

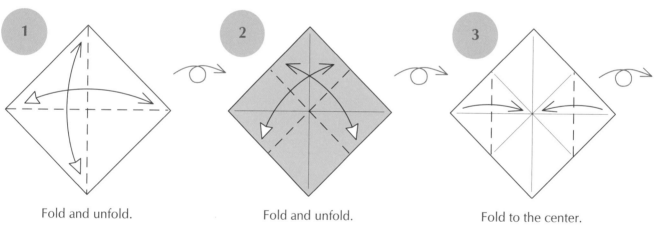

1 Fold and unfold.

2 Fold and unfold.

3 Fold to the center.

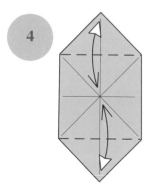

4 Fold to the center and unfold.

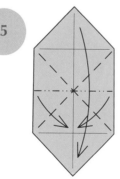

5 This is similar to the preliminary fold.

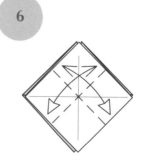

6 Fold and unfold the top layers. Repeat behind.

7 This is similar to the preliminary fold. Repeat behind.

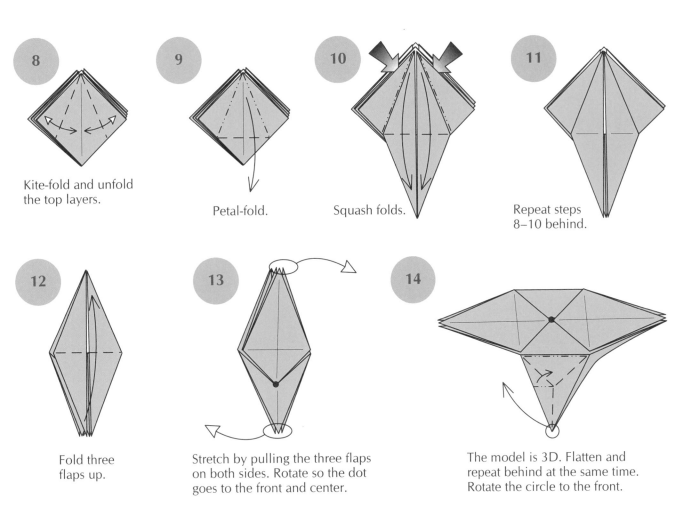

8 Kite-fold and unfold the top layers.

9 Petal-fold.

10 Squash folds.

11 Repeat steps 8–10 behind.

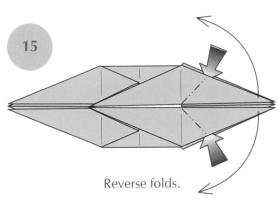

12 Fold three flaps up.

13 Stretch by pulling the three flaps on both sides. Rotate so the dot goes to the front and center.

14 The model is 3D. Flatten and repeat behind at the same time. Rotate the circle to the front.

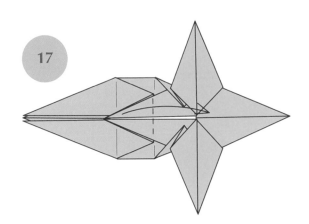

15 Reverse folds.

16 Squash folds.

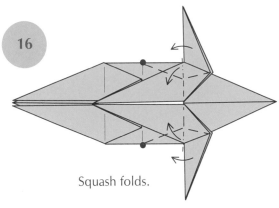

17

18 Pull out hidden paper from the center.

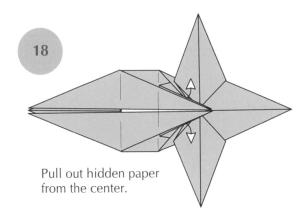

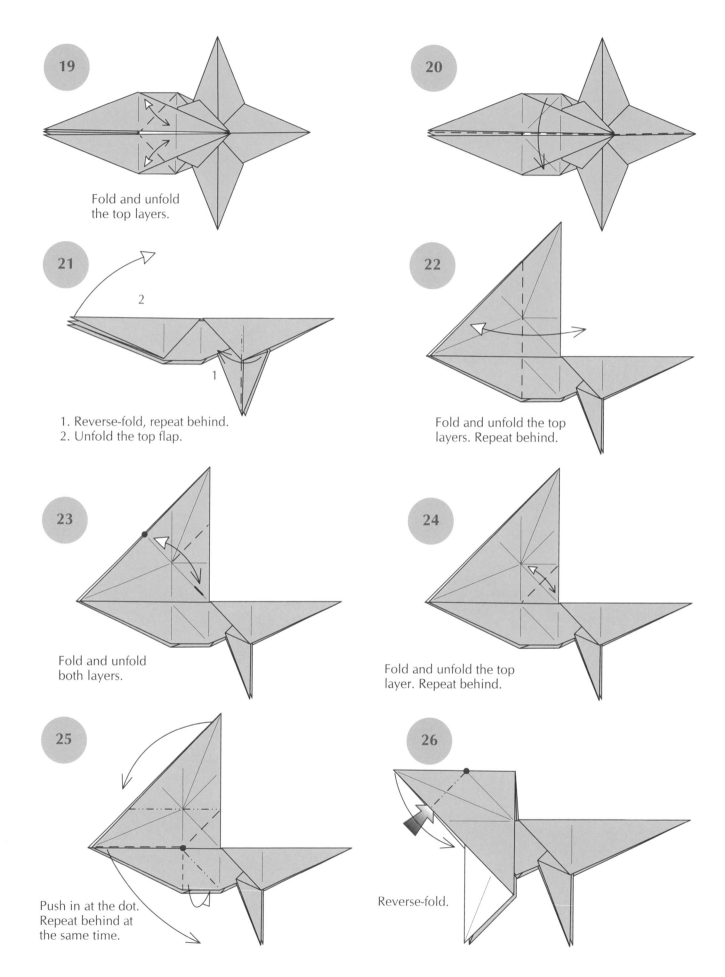

19 Fold and unfold the top layers.

20

21
1. Reverse-fold, repeat behind.
2. Unfold the top flap.

22 Fold and unfold the top layers. Repeat behind.

23 Fold and unfold both layers.

24 Fold and unfold the top layer. Repeat behind.

25 Push in at the dot. Repeat behind at the same time.

26 Reverse-fold.

27

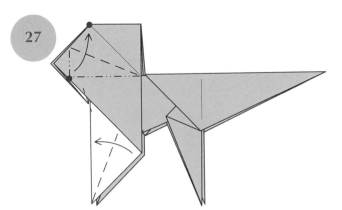

Petal-fold. Repeat behind.

28

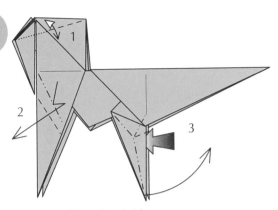

1. Fold and unfold.
2. Crimp-fold. Repeat behind at a different angle.
3. Double-rabbit-ear, repeat behind.

29

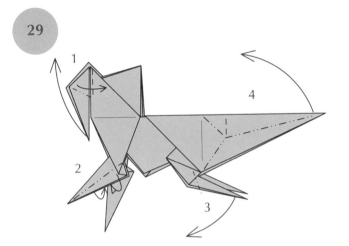

1. Crimp-fold.
2. Fold inside on both sides to thin the leg. Repeat behind.
3. Reverse-fold. Repeat behind at a different angle.
4. Double-rabbit-ear.

30

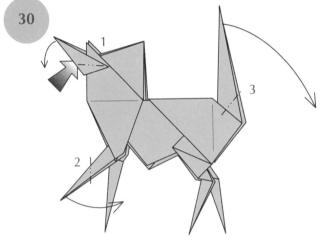

1. Open the head on both sides.
2. Reverse-fold.
3. Reverse-fold.

31

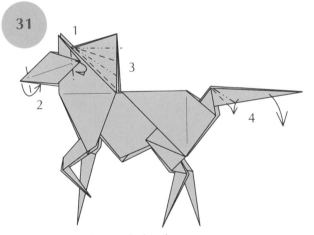

1. Repeat behind.
2. Reverse-fold.
3. Pleat the mane.
4. Spread the tail.

32

Horse

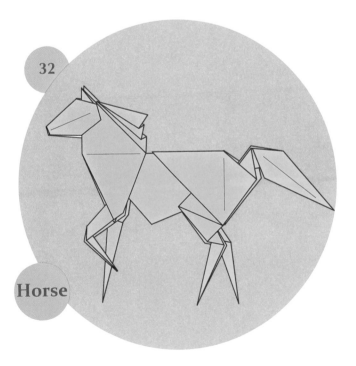

Horse

Designed by Fabian Correa G.
Colombia
Originally diagrammed by
Fabian Correa G.

http://www.flickr.com/
photos/fabiancorrea/

Horses have the largest eyes of any
land mammal. Placed on the sides
of their heads for a large panoramic
view, horses can see almost
completely around themselves. Their
blind spots are directly in front of
and directly behind them. Like most
mammals, they see only two colors
(similar to blue and yellow), but
their night vision is better than ours.
The wide view and keen night vision
is their adaptation as a prey animal.

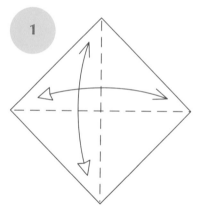

Fold and unfold.

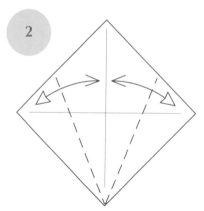

Kite-fold and unfold.

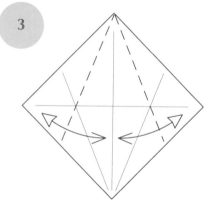

Kite-fold and unfold.

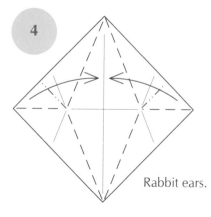

Rabbit ears.

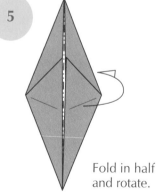

Fold in half
and rotate.

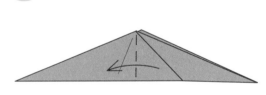

Repeat behind.

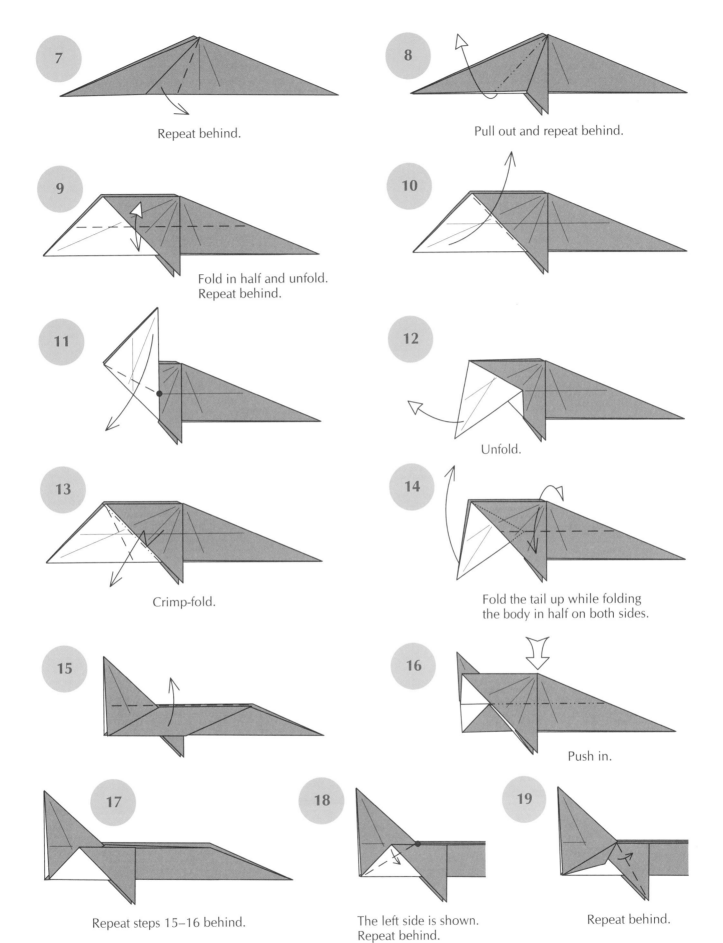

7 Repeat behind.

8 Pull out and repeat behind.

9 Fold in half and unfold. Repeat behind.

10

11

12 Unfold.

13 Crimp-fold.

14 Fold the tail up while folding the body in half on both sides.

15

16 Push in.

17 Repeat steps 15–16 behind.

18 The left side is shown. Repeat behind.

19 Repeat behind.

Horse 63

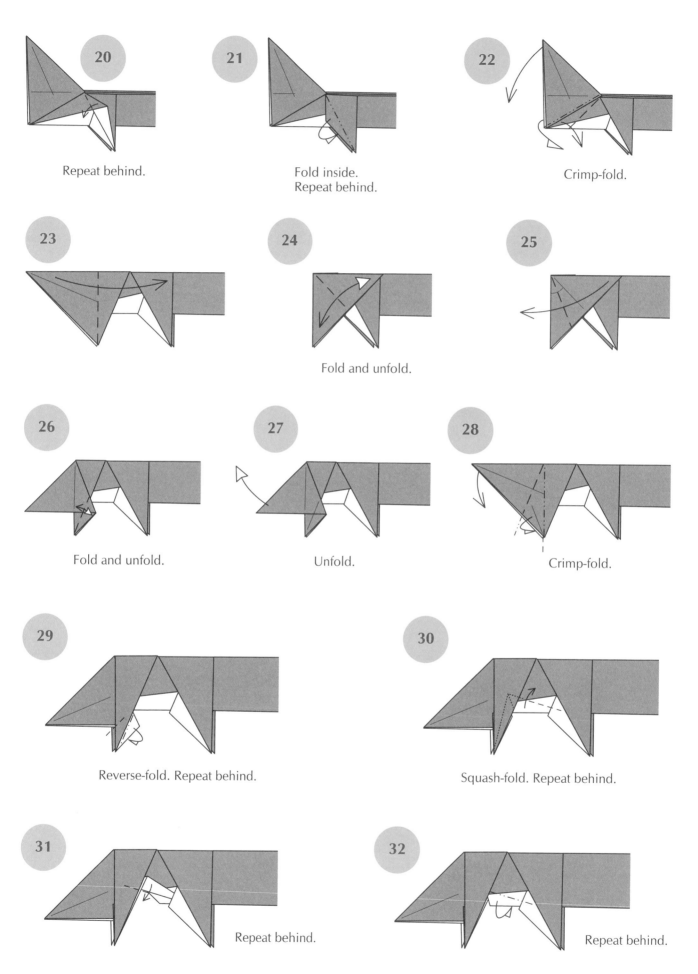

20 Repeat behind.

21 Fold inside. Repeat behind.

22 Crimp-fold.

23

24 Fold and unfold.

25

26 Fold and unfold.

27 Unfold.

28 Crimp-fold.

29 Reverse-fold. Repeat behind.

30 Squash-fold. Repeat behind.

31 Repeat behind.

32 Repeat behind.

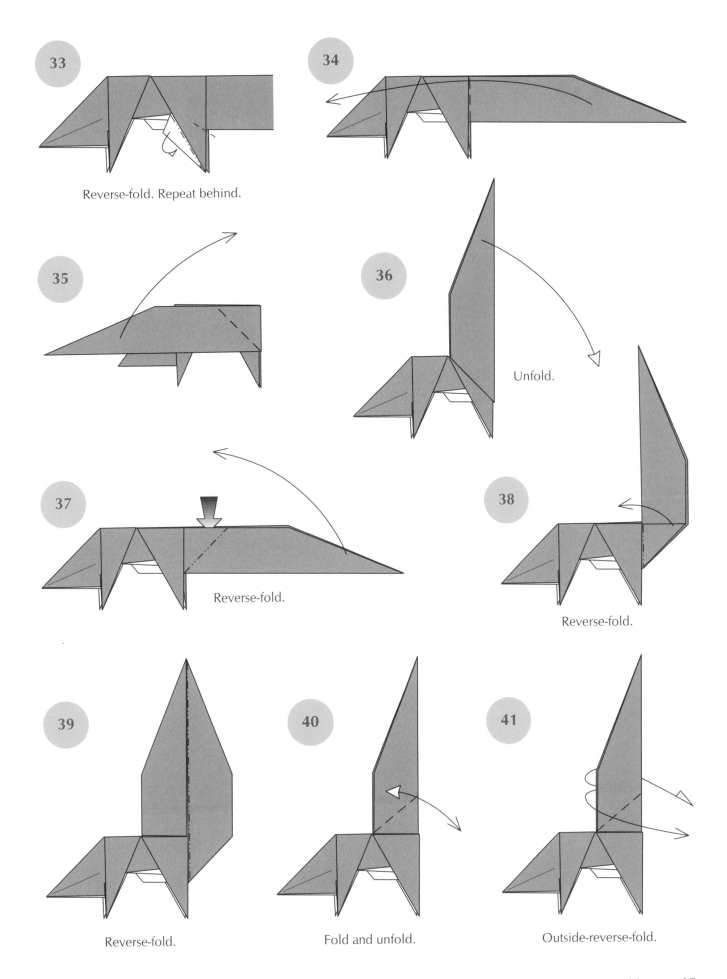

33 Reverse-fold. Repeat behind.

34

35

36 Unfold.

37 Reverse-fold.

38 Reverse-fold.

39 Reverse-fold.

40 Fold and unfold.

41 Outside-reverse-fold.

42 Bring the edge to the dot.

43 Unfold.

44 Reverse-fold.

45 Outside-reverse-fold.

46 Crimp-fold.

47
1. Reverse-fold.
2. Thin the legs, repeat behind.

48 Head.
1. Repeat behind.
2. Crimp-fold.

49 Shape the head.

50
1. Shape the back.
2. Fold the neck.

51 Shape the neck and tail.

52 **Horse**

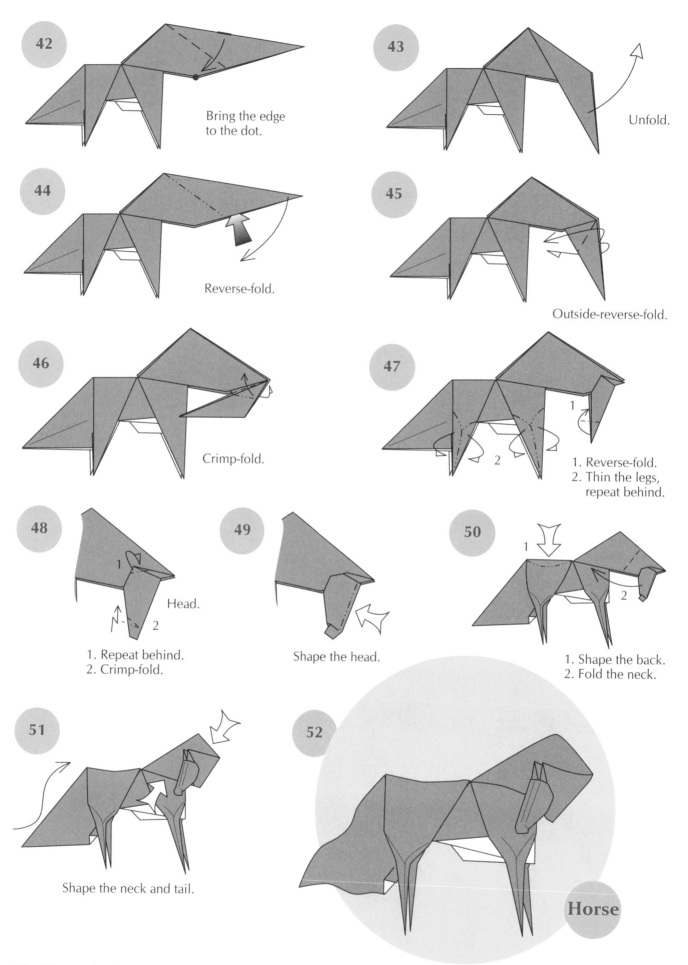

Horse

Designed by Gen Hagiwara
Japan
Originally diagrammed by
Gen Hagiwara

http://www.flickr.com/photos/
gen_hagiwara/

Horses spend 16-18 hours a
day grazing. They generally eat
grass and hay, eating small
amounts throughout the day.
Horses need only about two
and a half hours of sleep per
day, spread out in short
intervals. They can sleep both
standing up and lying down.

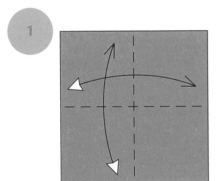

Fold and unfold.

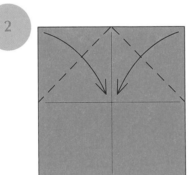

Fold to the center.

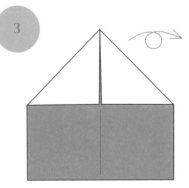

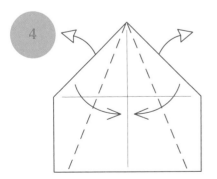

Fold to the center and
swing out from behind.

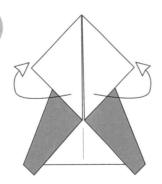

Unfold back to step 3.

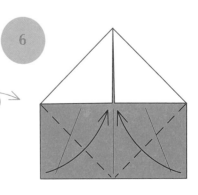

Fold to the center.

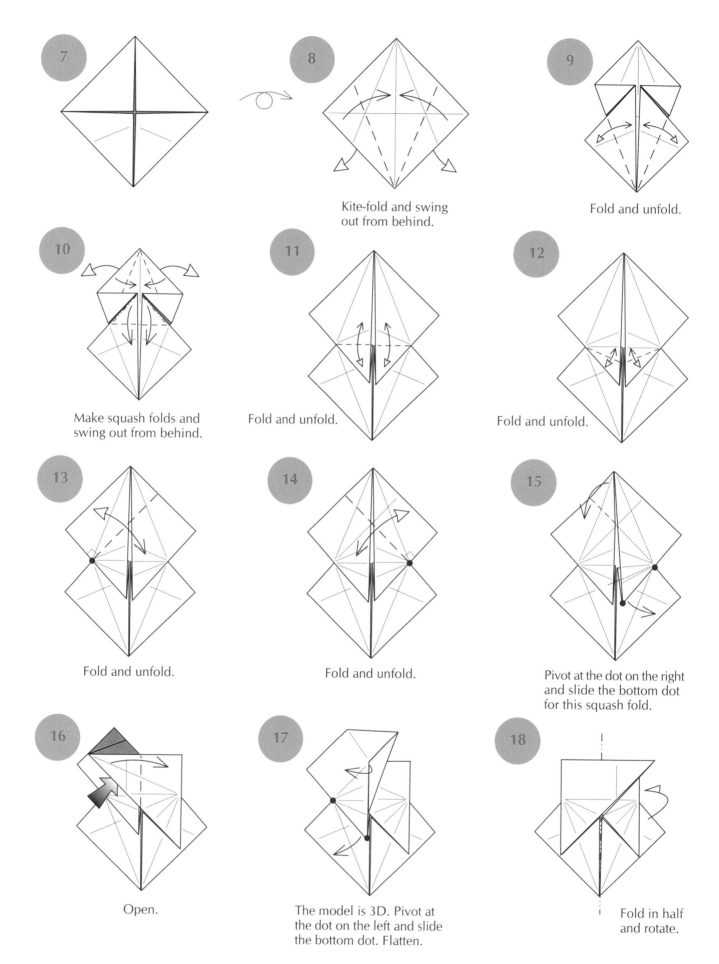

7

8

Kite-fold and swing
out from behind.

9

Fold and unfold.

10

Make squash folds and
swing out from behind.

11

Fold and unfold.

12

Fold and unfold.

13

Fold and unfold.

14

Fold and unfold.

15

Pivot at the dot on the right
and slide the bottom dot
for this squash fold.

16

Open.

17

The model is 3D. Pivot at
the dot on the left and slide
the bottom dot. Flatten.

18

Fold in half
and rotate.

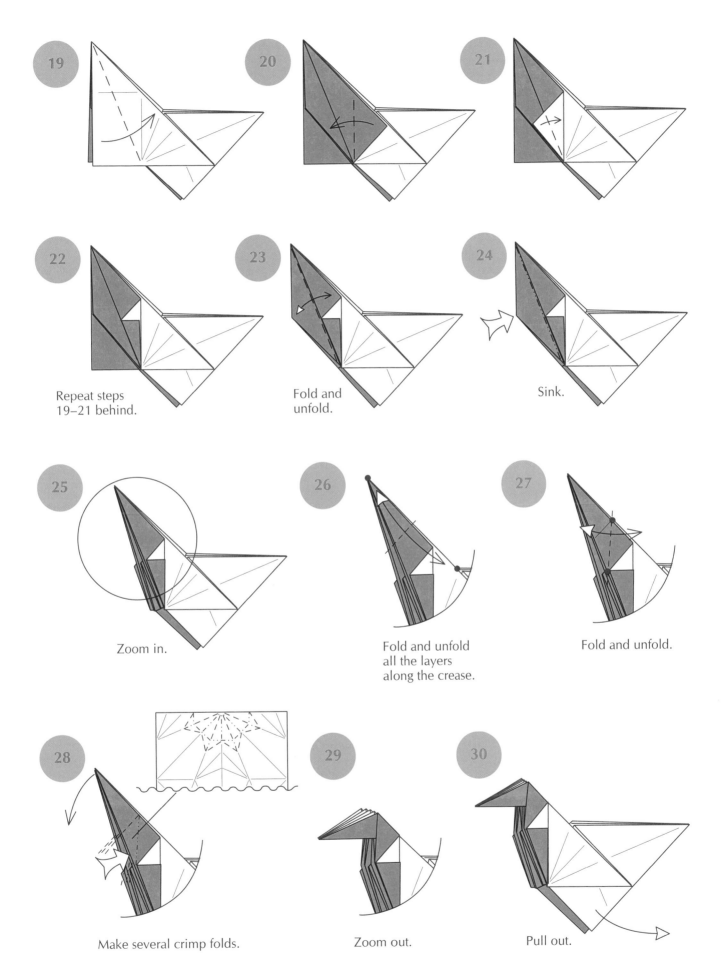

19

20

21

22

Repeat steps
19–21 behind.

23

Fold and
unfold.

24

Sink.

25

Zoom in.

26

Fold and unfold
all the layers
along the crease.

27

Fold and unfold.

28

Make several crimp folds.

29

Zoom out.

30

Pull out.

Horse 69

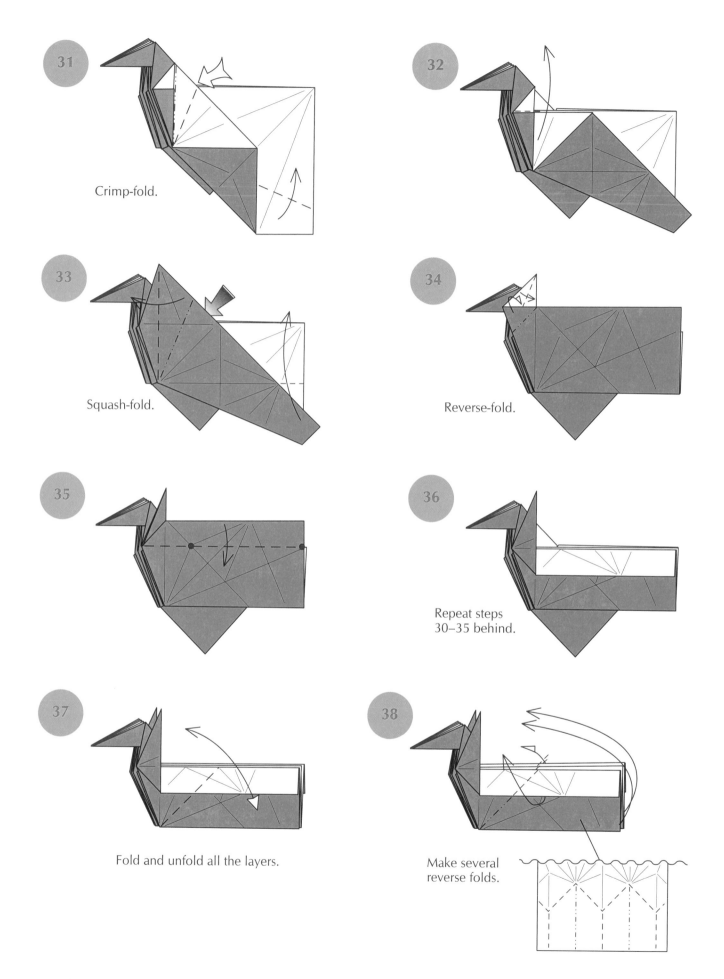

31 Crimp-fold.

32

33 Squash-fold.

34 Reverse-fold.

35

36 Repeat steps 30–35 behind.

37 Fold and unfold all the layers.

38 Make several reverse folds.

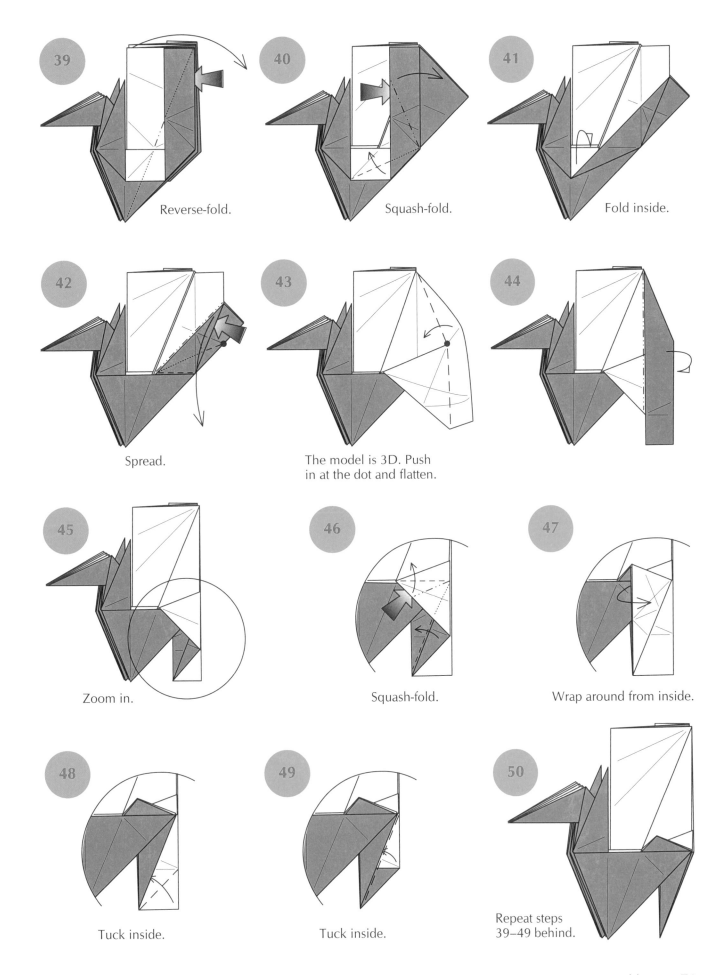

39 Reverse-fold.

40 Squash-fold.

41 Fold inside.

42 Spread.

43 The model is 3D. Push in at the dot and flatten.

44

45 Zoom in.

46 Squash-fold.

47 Wrap around from inside.

48 Tuck inside.

49 Tuck inside.

50 Repeat steps 39–49 behind.

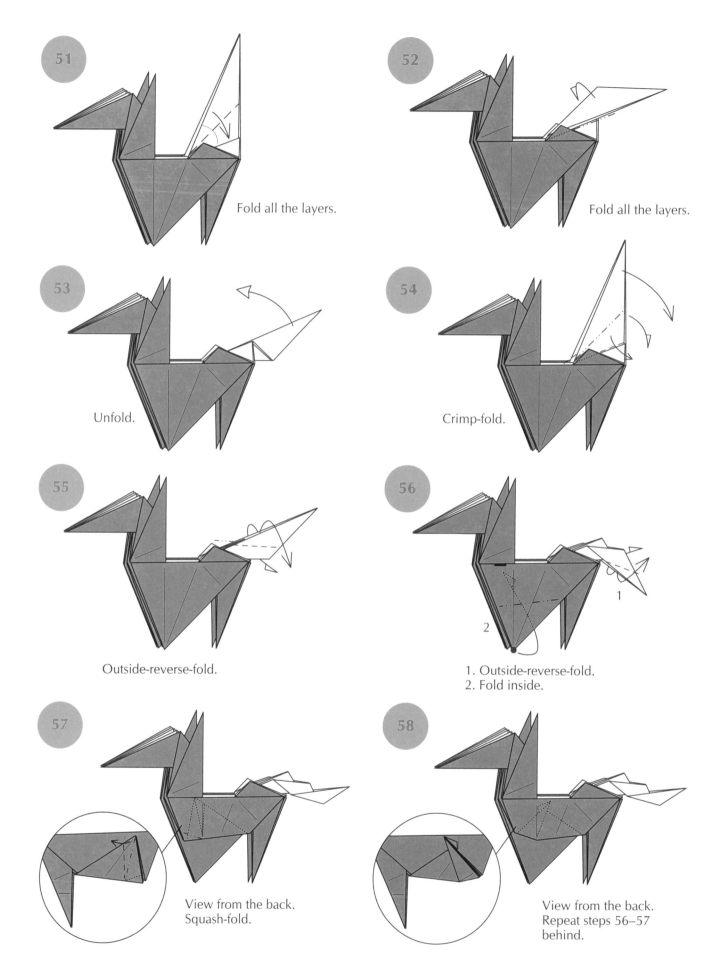

51 Fold all the layers.

52 Fold all the layers.

53 Unfold.

54 Crimp-fold.

55 Outside-reverse-fold.

56
1. Outside-reverse-fold.
2. Fold inside.

57 View from the back. Squash-fold.

58 View from the back. Repeat steps 56–57 behind.

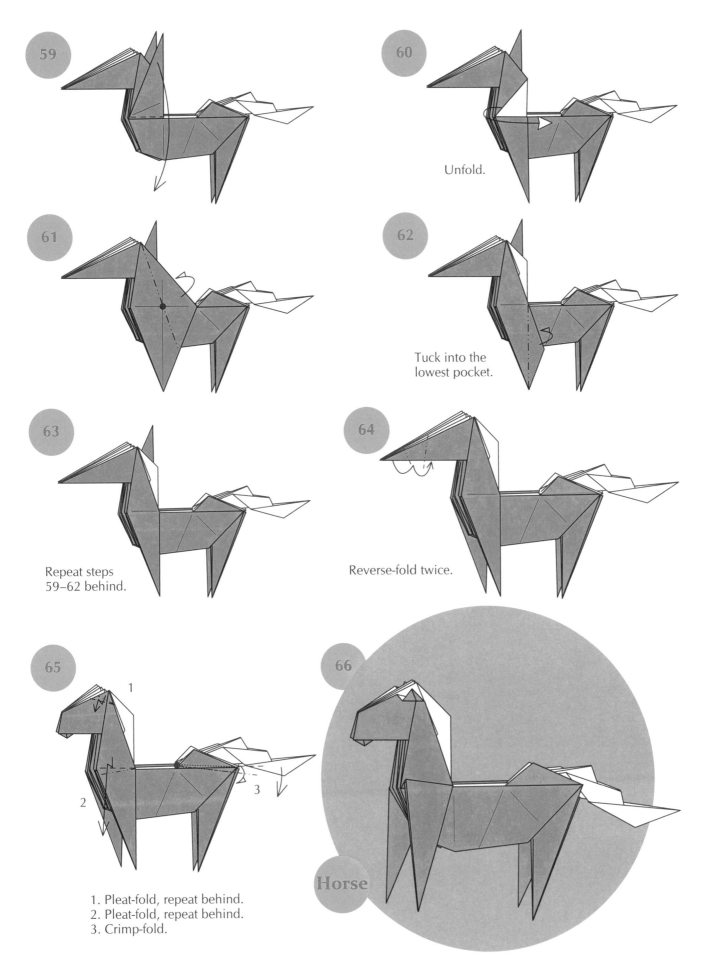

59

60

Unfold.

61

62

Tuck into the
lowest pocket.

63

Repeat steps
59–62 behind.

64

Reverse-fold twice.

65

1. Pleat-fold, repeat behind.
2. Pleat-fold, repeat behind.
3. Crimp-fold.

66

Horse

Fantasy

The horse has qualities unlike any animal. Many mythological beasts, therefore, are an extension of the power and elegance of this humble creature. Here is a collection of horse-themed fantasy creatures in origami.

Pegasus

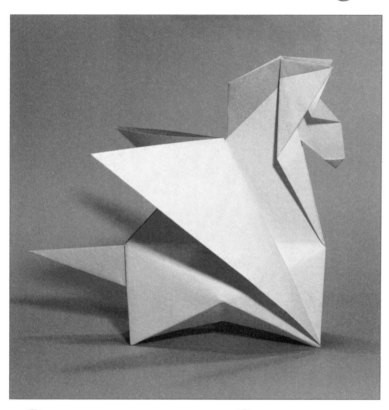

Designed by Jacky Chan
Hong Kong
Originally diagrammed by Jacky Chan

http://www.jackychan.org/

Pegasus is the winged flying horse from Greek mythology. Often shown as a white creature, Pegasus was mysterious and gentle, always ready to help.

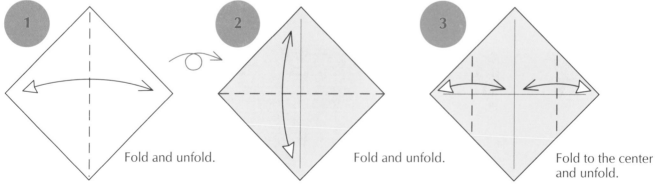

1. Fold and unfold.

2. Fold and unfold.

3. Fold to the center and unfold.

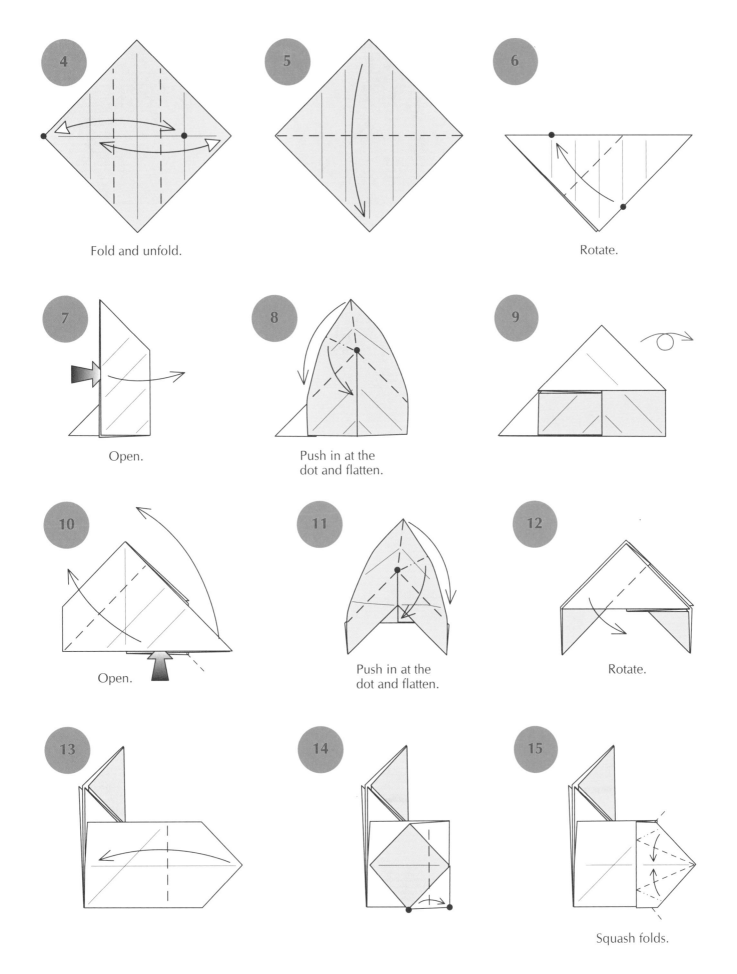

4 Fold and unfold.

5

6 Rotate.

7 Open.

8 Push in at the dot and flatten.

9

10 Open.

11 Push in at the dot and flatten.

12 Rotate.

13

14

15 Squash folds.

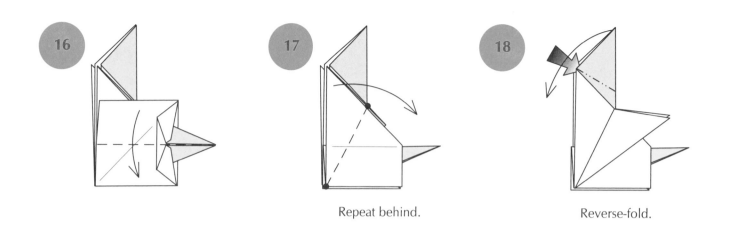

16

17
Repeat behind.

18
Reverse-fold.

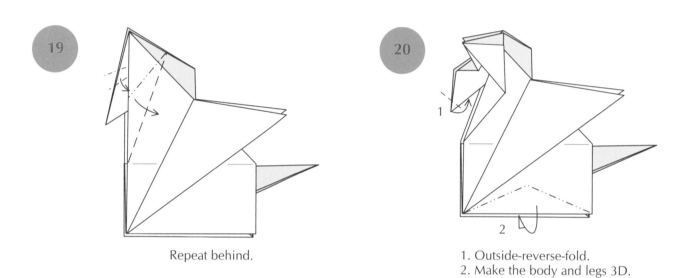

19
Repeat behind.

20
1. Outside-reverse-fold.
2. Make the body and legs 3D.
   Repeat behind.

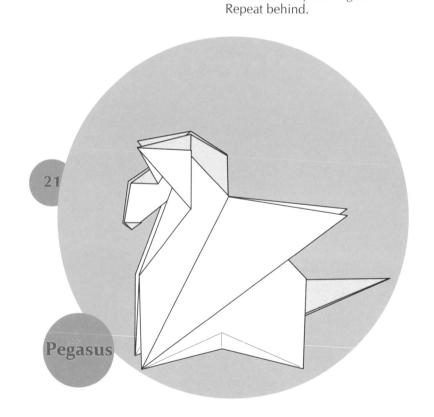

21

Pegasus

Pegasus

Designed by John Montroll

Pegasus is a symbol of knowledge, glory, beauty, artistic inspiration, and soaring to great heights without limit.

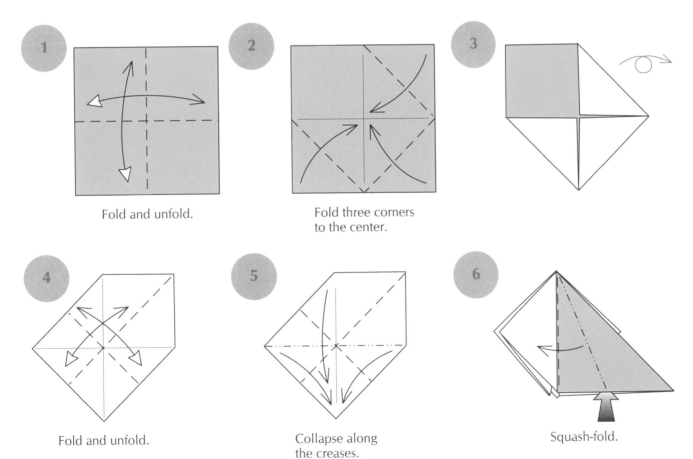

1 Fold and unfold.

2 Fold three corners to the center.

3

4 Fold and unfold.

5 Collapse along the creases.

6 Squash-fold.

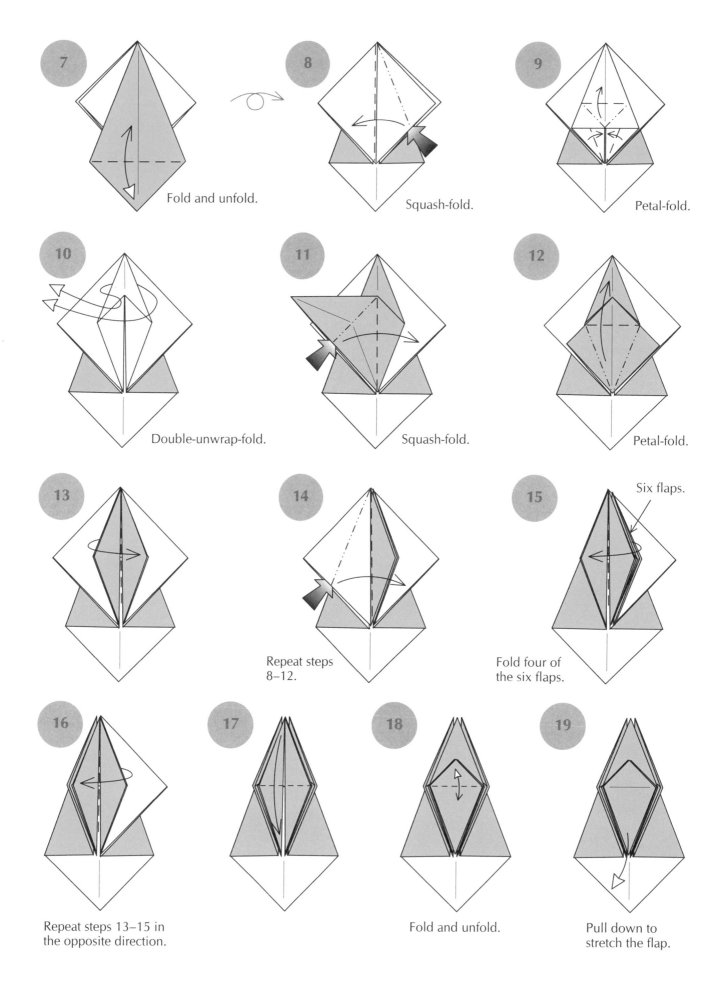

7 Fold and unfold.

8 Squash-fold.

9 Petal-fold.

10 Double-unwrap-fold.

11 Squash-fold.

12 Petal-fold.

13

14 Repeat steps 8–12.

15 Six flaps. Fold four of the six flaps.

16 Repeat steps 13–15 in the opposite direction.

17

18 Fold and unfold.

19 Pull down to stretch the flap.

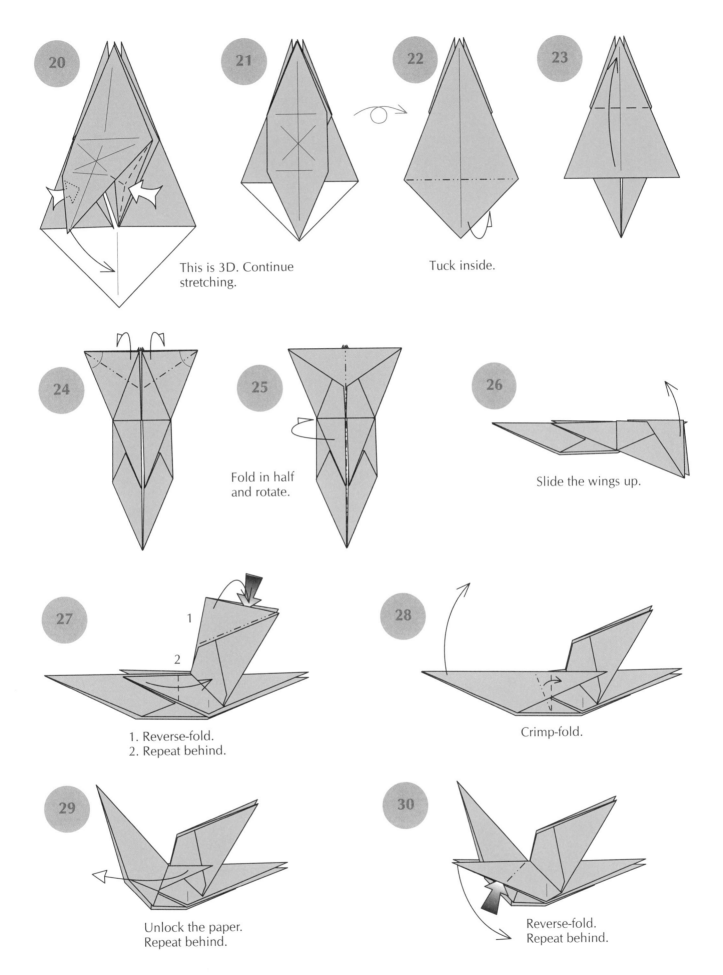

20 This is 3D. Continue stretching.

21

22 Tuck inside.

23

24

25 Fold in half and rotate.

26 Slide the wings up.

27 1. Reverse-fold.
2. Repeat behind.

28 Crimp-fold.

29 Unlock the paper. Repeat behind.

30 Reverse-fold. Repeat behind.

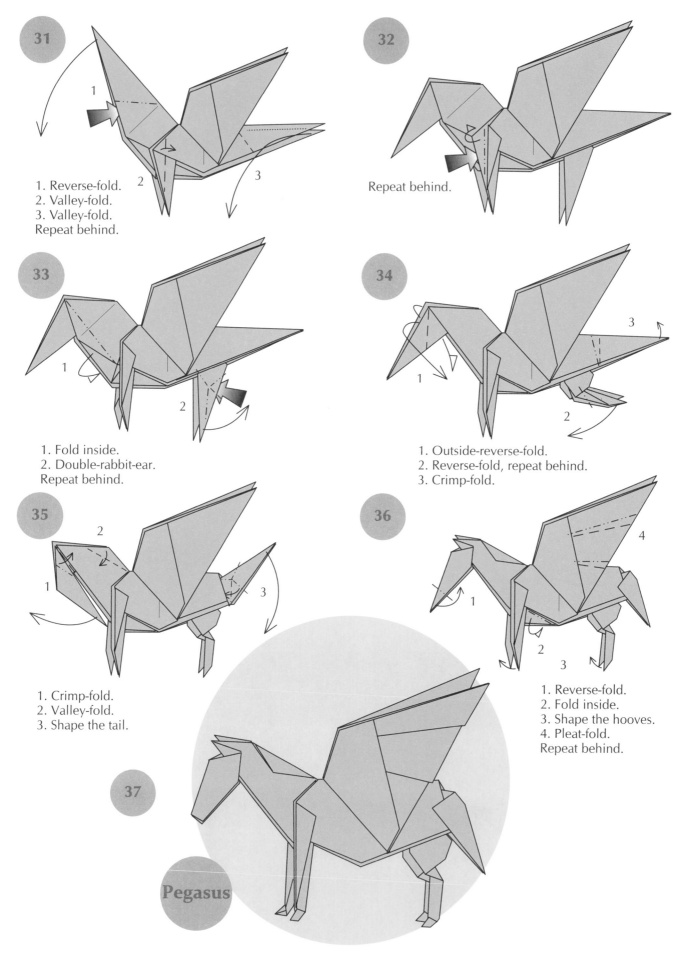

31

1. Reverse-fold.
2. Valley-fold.
3. Valley-fold.
Repeat behind.

32

Repeat behind.

33

1. Fold inside.
2. Double-rabbit-ear.
Repeat behind.

34

1. Outside-reverse-fold.
2. Reverse-fold, repeat behind.
3. Crimp-fold.

35

1. Crimp-fold.
2. Valley-fold.
3. Shape the tail.

36

1. Reverse-fold.
2. Fold inside.
3. Shape the hooves.
4. Pleat-fold.
Repeat behind.

37

Pegasus

Unicorn

Designed by Román Díaz
Uruguay

Originally diagrammed by
Román Díaz

The unicorn is depicted as
a white horse with a long
spiraling horn and a goat's
beard. It is a symbol of
magic, travel, and wisdom.
The horn is said to possess
healing powers.

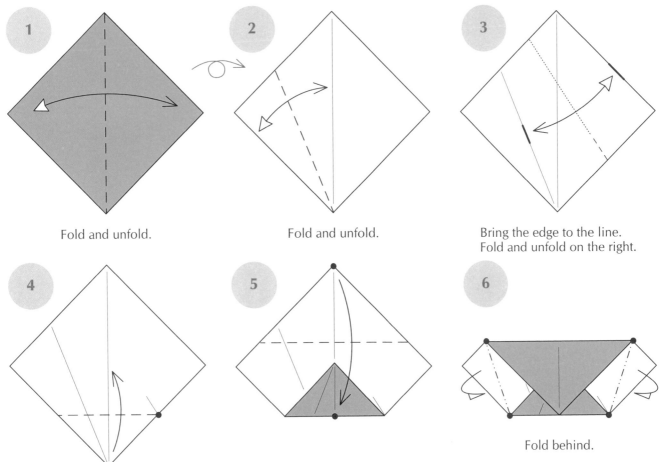

1 Fold and unfold.

2 Fold and unfold.

3 Bring the edge to the line.
Fold and unfold on the right.

4

5

6 Fold behind.

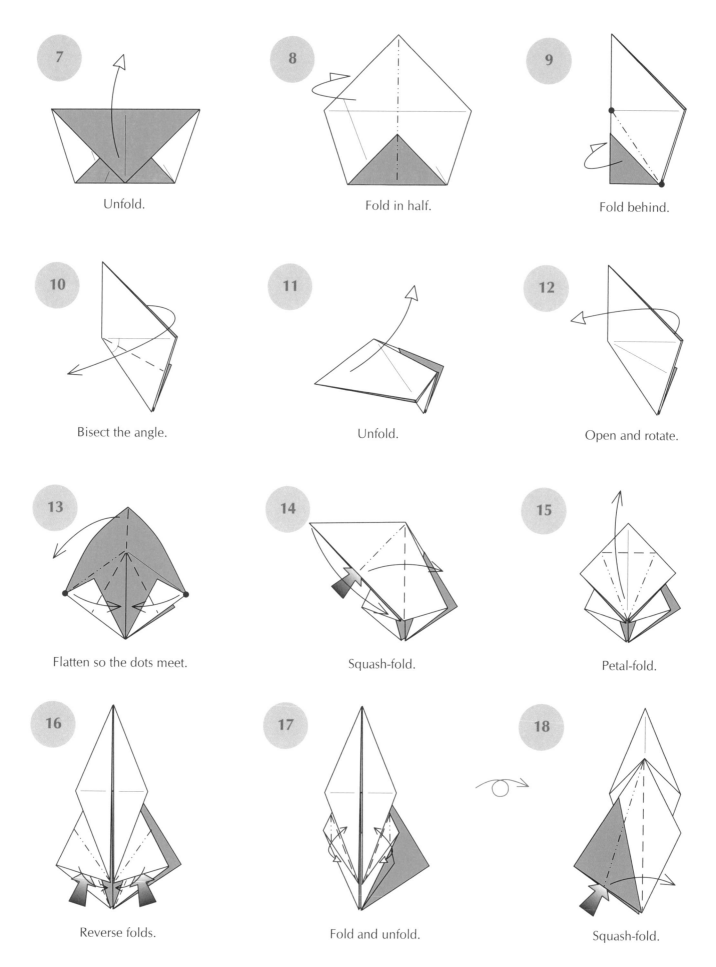

7 Unfold.

8 Fold in half.

9 Fold behind.

10 Bisect the angle.

11 Unfold.

12 Open and rotate.

13 Flatten so the dots meet.

14 Squash-fold.

15 Petal-fold.

16 Reverse folds.

17 Fold and unfold.

18 Squash-fold.

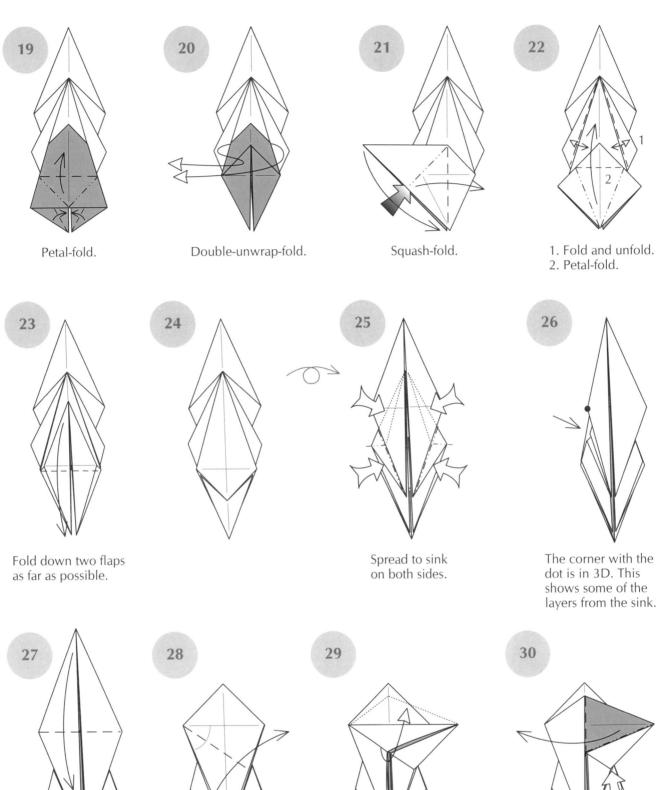

19

Petal-fold.

20

Double-unwrap-fold.

21

Squash-fold.

22

1. Fold and unfold.
2. Petal-fold.

23

Fold down two flaps
as far as possible.

24

25

Spread to sink
on both sides.

26

The corner with the
dot is in 3D. This
shows some of the
layers from the sink.

27

Fold one flap down.

28

Bisect the angle.

29

Pull out some
trapped paper.

30

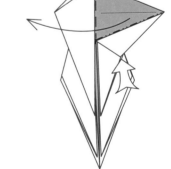

Fold the point to the left
while squash-folding the
bottom corner.

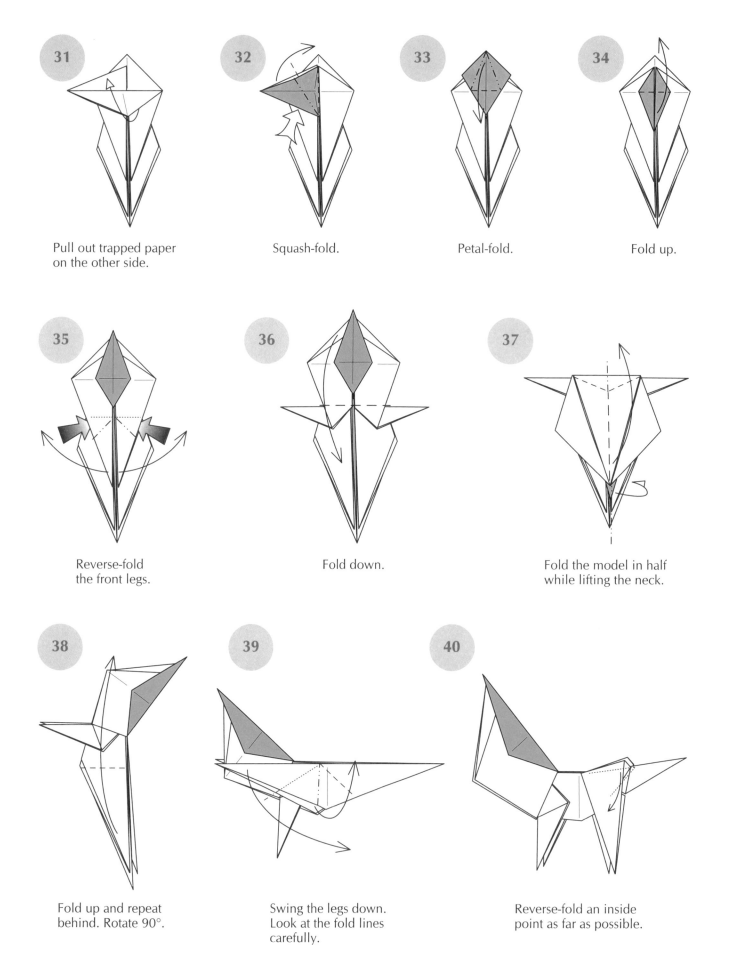

31 Pull out trapped paper on the other side.

32 Squash-fold.

33 Petal-fold.

34 Fold up.

35 Reverse-fold the front legs.

36 Fold down.

37 Fold the model in half while lifting the neck.

38 Fold up and repeat behind. Rotate 90°.

39 Swing the legs down. Look at the fold lines carefully.

40 Reverse-fold an inside point as far as possible.

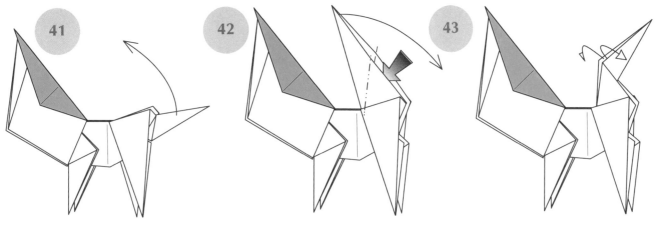

41 Swing the tail up as far as possible.

42 Reverse-fold the tail.

43 Carefully wrap a layer around the tail to color-change it. Repeat behind.

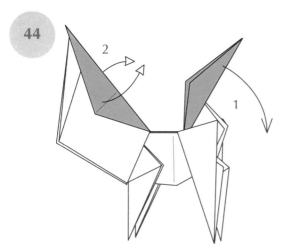

44
1. Slide the tail down.
2. Unfold at the mane.
Repeat behind.

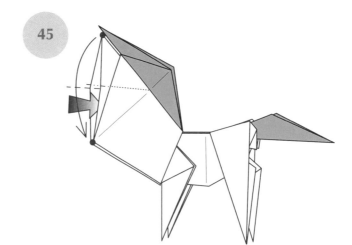

45 Reverse-fold.

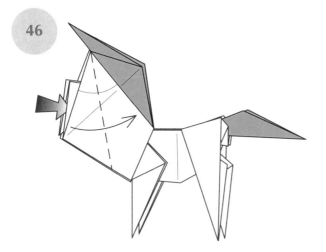

46 Bisect the angle while partially opening a corner. Repeat behind.

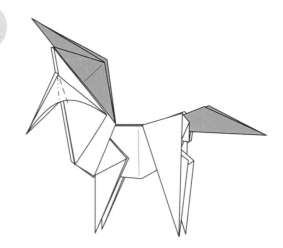

47 Flatten with a pleat. Repeat behind.

48

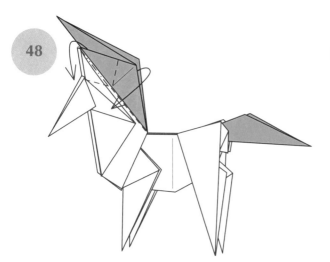

Valley-fold the mane with a
reverse fold. Repeat behind.

49

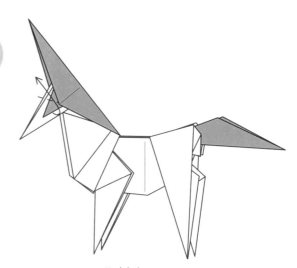

Fold the ears up.
Repeat behind.

50

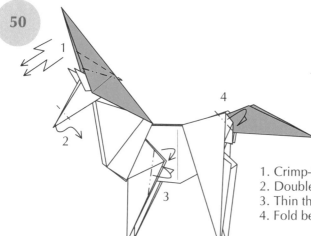

1. Crimp-fold to form the mane and horn.
2. Double reverse-fold the tip of the head.
3. Thin the front legs, repeat behind.
4. Fold behind, repeat behind.

51

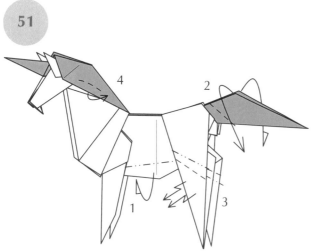

1. Fold behind.
2. Outside-reverse-fold the tail.
3. Crimp-fold the hind legs.
4. Shape the mane.
Repeat behind.

52

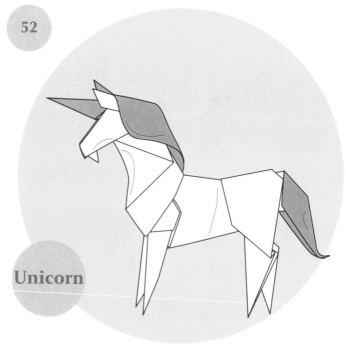

Unicorn

Centaur

Designed by Peter Budai
Hungary
Originally diagrammed by Peter Budai

http://www.budaiorigami.hu

The Centaur, half-man and half-horse, is a creature from Greek mythology. Being both animal and human, it symbolizes duality; intellect and instinct, conflict between body and mind, good and evil.

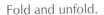

1

Fold and unfold.

2

Fold and unfold.

3

Fold to the center.

4

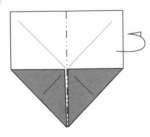

Fold in half and rotate 90°.

5

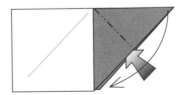

Reverse-fold.

6

Squash-fold.

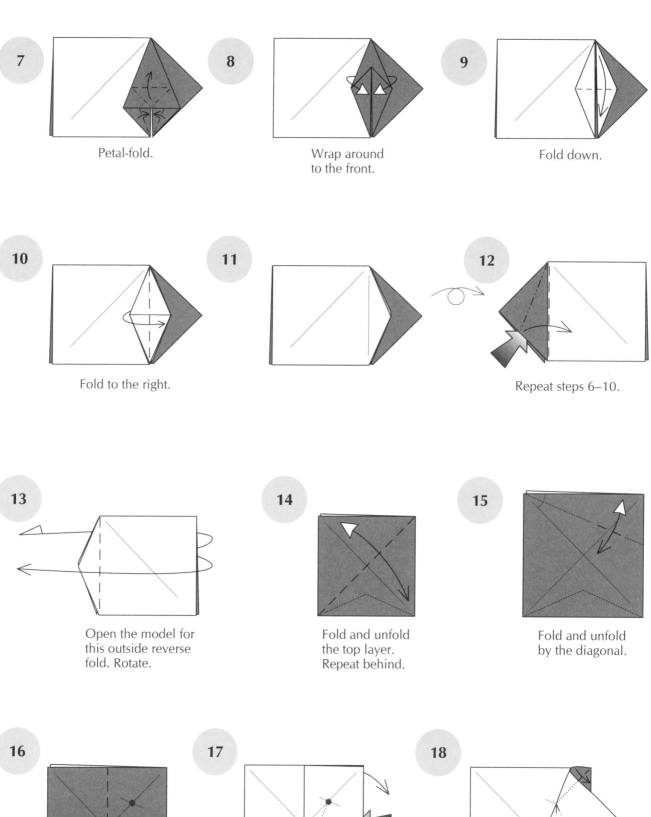

7 Petal-fold.

8 Wrap around to the front.

9 Fold down.

10 Fold to the right.

11

12 Repeat steps 6–10.

13 Open the model for this outside reverse fold. Rotate.

14 Fold and unfold the top layer. Repeat behind.

15 Fold and unfold by the diagonal.

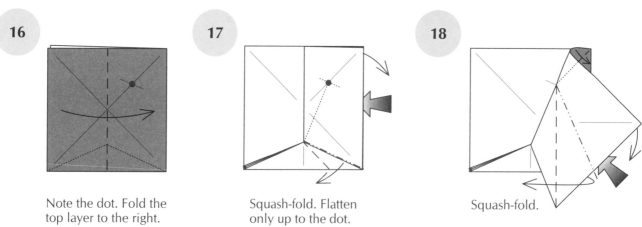

16 Note the dot. Fold the top layer to the right.

17 Squash-fold. Flatten only up to the dot.

18 Squash-fold.

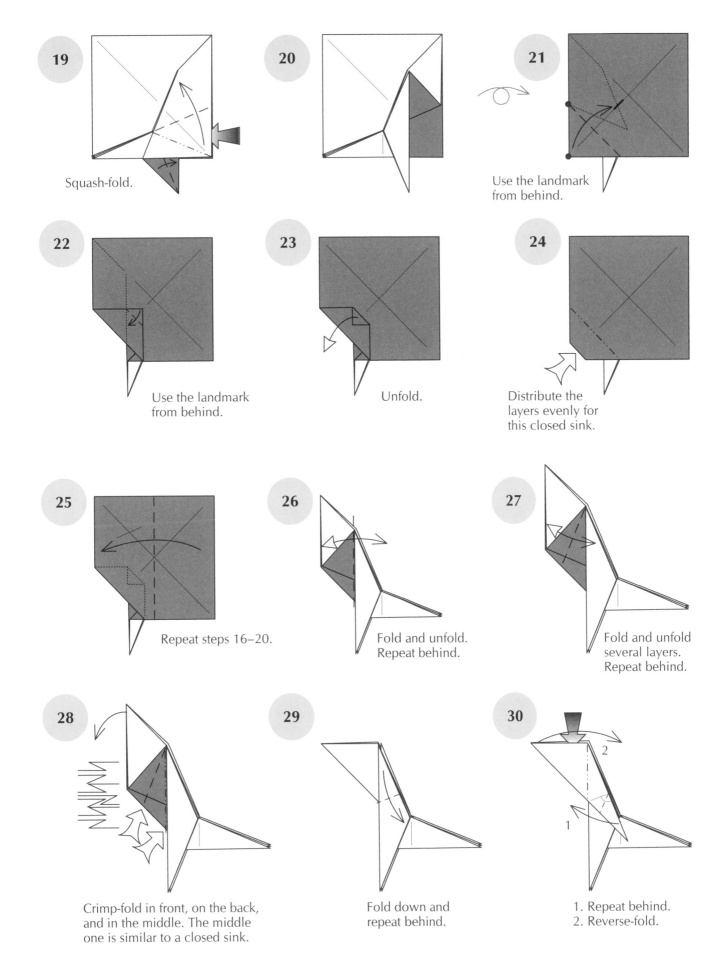

19 Squash-fold.

20

21 Use the landmark from behind.

22 Use the landmark from behind.

23 Unfold.

24 Distribute the layers evenly for this closed sink.

25 Repeat steps 16–20.

26 Fold and unfold. Repeat behind.

27 Fold and unfold several layers. Repeat behind.

28 Crimp-fold in front, on the back, and in the middle. The middle one is similar to a closed sink.

29 Fold down and repeat behind.

30 1. Repeat behind. 2. Reverse-fold.

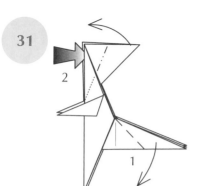

1. Repeat behind.
2. Reverse-fold.

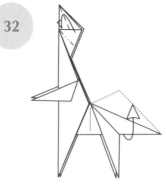

1. Pull out the top two layers.
2. Reverse-fold.
Repeat behind.

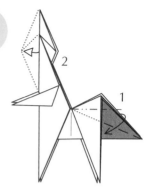

1. Squash-fold the top layer.
2. Pull out.
Repeat behind.

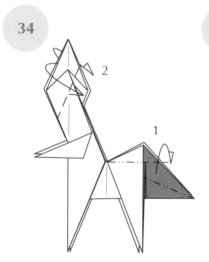

1. Squash-fold into the center.
   Repeat behind.
2. Outside-reverse-fold.

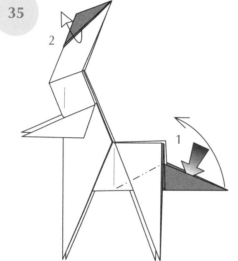

1. Reverse-fold.
2. Reveal some trapped paper,
   it could be on either side.

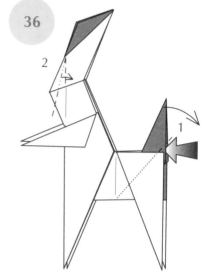

1. Reverse-fold.
2. Squash-fold,
   repeat behind.

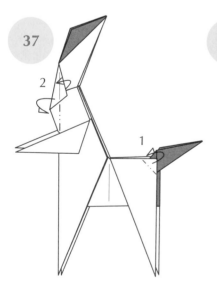

1. Mountain-fold the corner.
2. Swing.
Repeat behind.

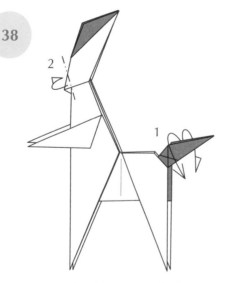

1. Outside-reverse-fold.
2. Mountain-fold,
   repeat behind.

This is similar
to a crimp fold.

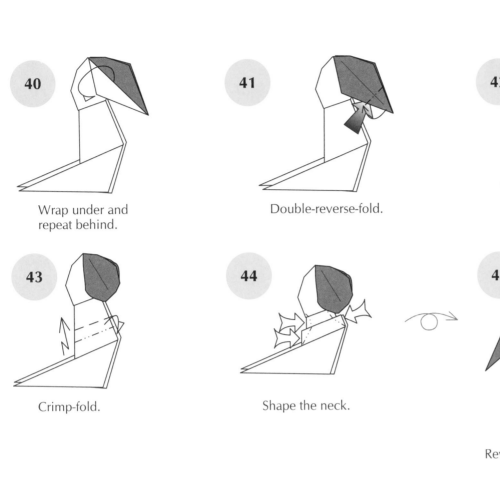

40

Wrap under and repeat behind.

41

Double-reverse-fold.

42

Shape the hair.

43

Crimp-fold.

44

Shape the neck.

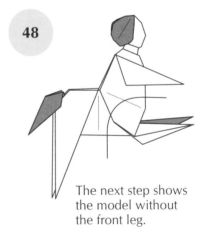

45

Reverse-fold and repeat behind.

46

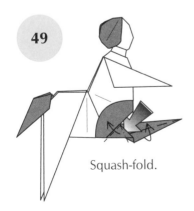

Fold up and repeat on the other leg.

47

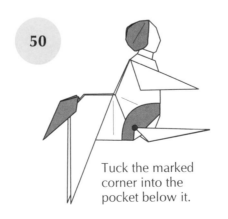

Mountain-fold and repeat on the other leg.

48

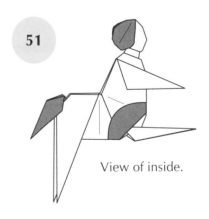

The next step shows the model without the front leg.

49

Squash-fold.

50

Tuck the marked corner into the pocket below it.

51

View of inside.

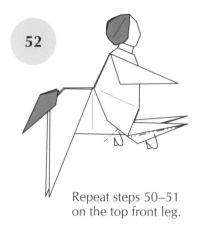

52 Repeat steps 50–51 on the top front leg.

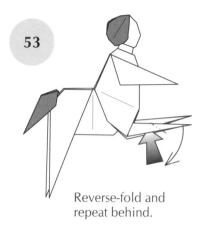

53 Reverse-fold and repeat behind.

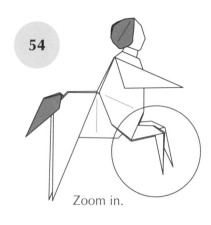

54 Zoom in.

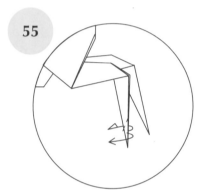

55 Outside-reverse-fold and repeat behind.

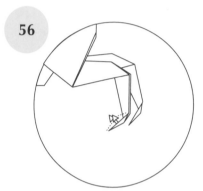

56 Pull out some paper to make the hoof. Repeat behind.

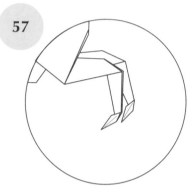

57 Zoom in for the next step.

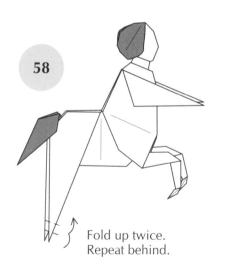

58 Fold up twice. Repeat behind.

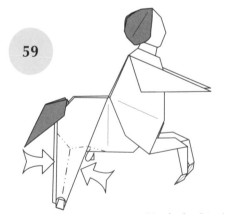

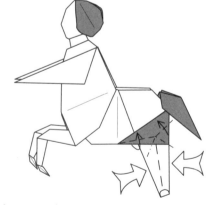

59 Pinch the hind legs together with a rabbit ear inside.

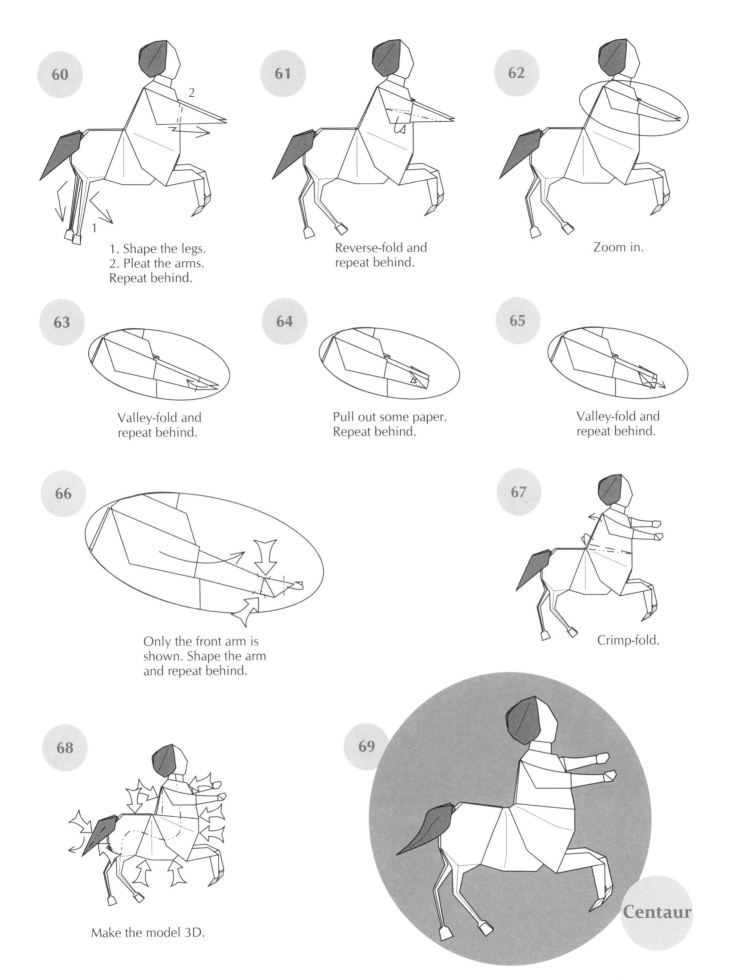

60

1. Shape the legs.
2. Pleat the arms.
Repeat behind.

61

Reverse-fold and
repeat behind.

62

Zoom in.

63

Valley-fold and
repeat behind.

64

Pull out some paper.
Repeat behind.

65

Valley-fold and
repeat behind.

66

Only the front arm is
shown. Shape the arm
and repeat behind.

67

Crimp-fold.

68

Make the model 3D.

69

Centaur

Horse Breeds

Horse breeds are divided into three general categories. "Coldbloods," such as the Clydesdale, are gentle, larger horses capable of heavy work. "Hotbloods," such as the Thoroughbred, are spirited, fast horses. "Warmbloods," such as the Lipizzan, are for riding and equestrian sports. Today, there are over 300 breeds worldwide.

Quarter Horse

Designed by John Montroll

The Quarter Horse, named for its speed and ability when racing the quarter mile, is a fixture at racetrack and rodeo events, and is equally suited for farm work, where it serves to watch and work with cows. Intelligent and gentle, Quarter Horses are a good choice for trail riding.

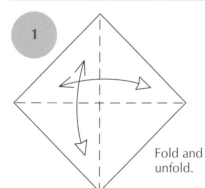

1

Fold and unfold.

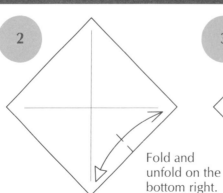

2

Fold and unfold on the bottom right.

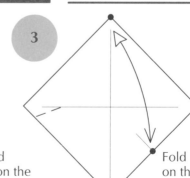

3

Fold and unfold on the left so the dots meet.

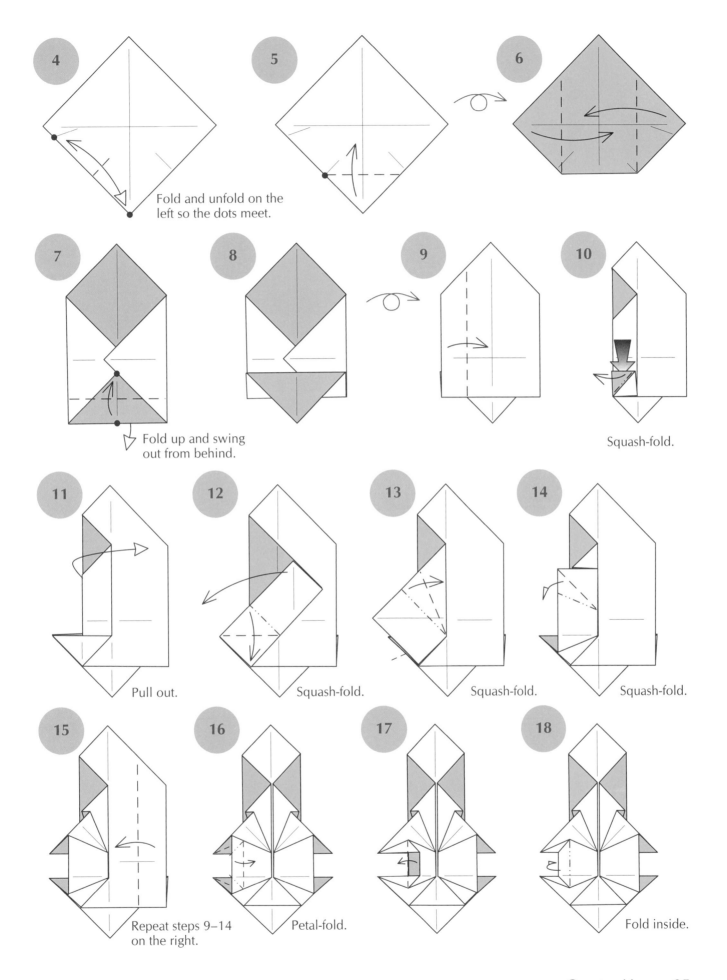

4 Fold and unfold on the left so the dots meet.

5

6

7 Fold up and swing out from behind.

8

9

10 Squash-fold.

11 Pull out.

12 Squash-fold.

13 Squash-fold.

14 Squash-fold.

15 Repeat steps 9–14 on the right.

16 Petal-fold.

17

18 Fold inside.

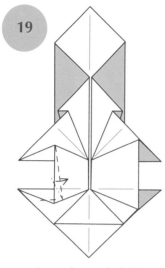

19

Spread-squash-fold.

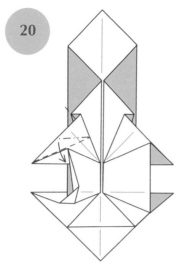

20

Squash-fold.

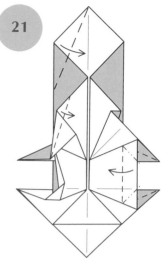

21

Repeat steps 16–21 on the right.

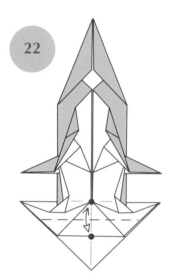

22

Fold and unfold.

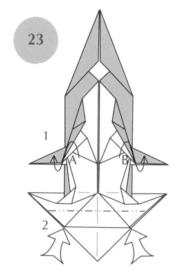

23

1. Bring regions A and B to the top layer.
2. Sink.

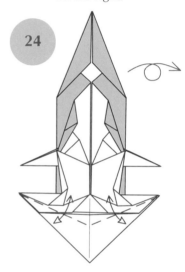

24

Fold and unfold.

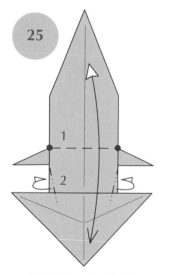

25

1. Fold and unfold.
2. Fold inside.

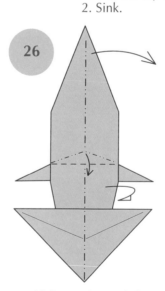

26

Fold the neck up while folding in half. Rotate.

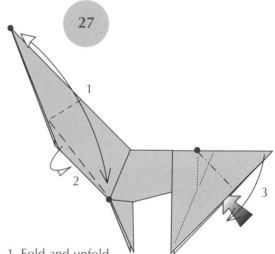

27

1. Fold and unfold.
2. Repeat behind.
3. Reverse-fold.

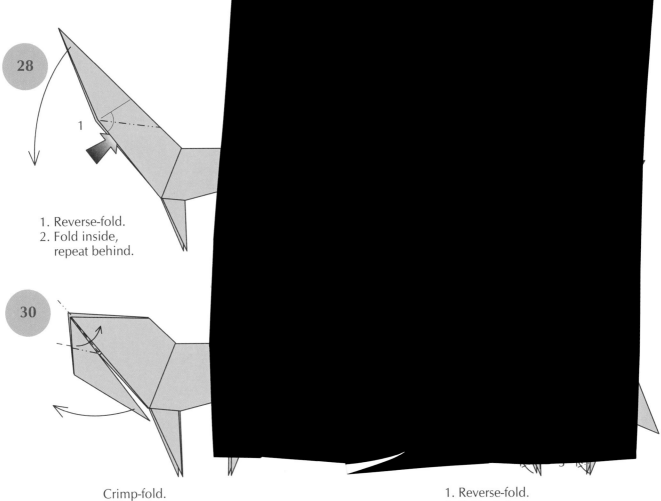

28

1. Reverse-fold.
2. Fold inside,
   repeat behind.

30

Crimp-fold.

1. Reverse-fold.
2. Fold all the layers.
3. Squash folds, repeat behind.

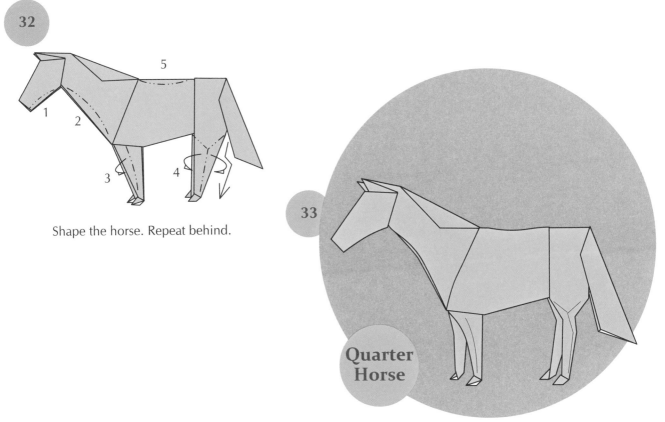

32

Shape the horse. Repeat behind.

33

Quarter
Horse

Designed by John Montroll

Named for an old town in Scotland, Clydesdale Horses are well suited to heavy labor such as pulling carts and farm work due to their strength and solidity of body. Their distinctive hairy, thick lower legs make them easy to identify in popular television advertisements.

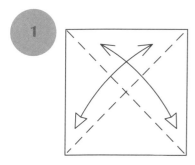

Fold and unfold.

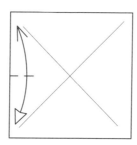

Fold and unfold on the left.

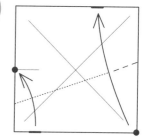

Bring the bottom edge to the dot on the left and the lower right corner to the top edge. Crease on the right.

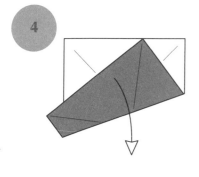

Unfold.

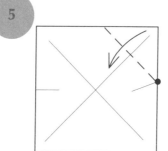

Rotate.

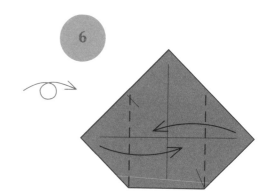

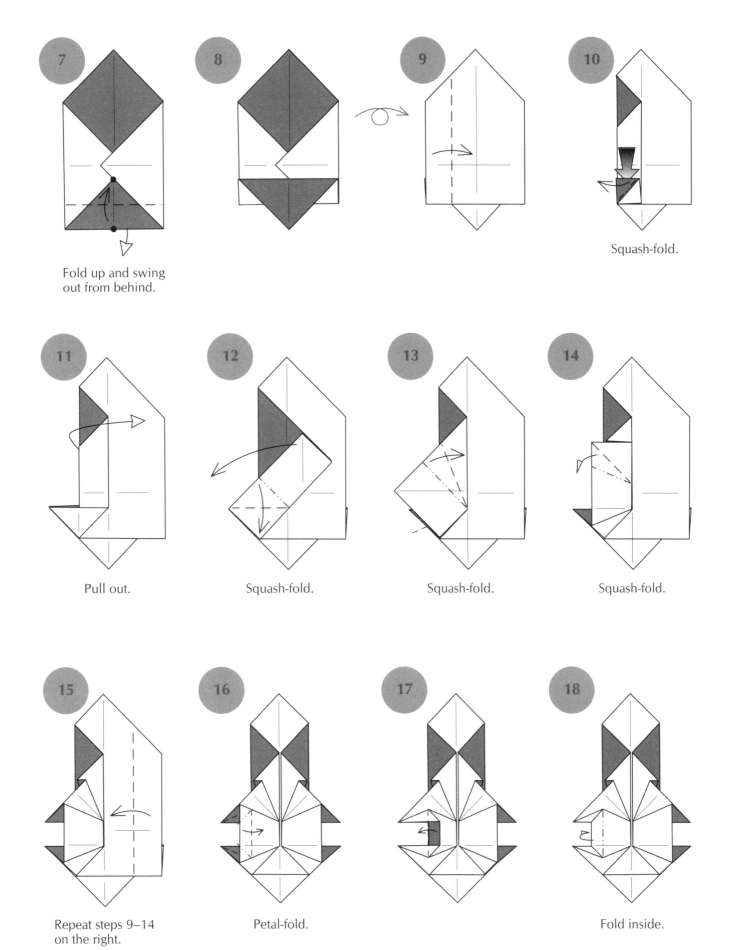

7

Fold up and swing out from behind.

8

9

10

Squash-fold.

11

Pull out.

12

Squash-fold.

13

Squash-fold.

14

Squash-fold.

15

Repeat steps 9–14 on the right.

16

Petal-fold.

17

18

Fold inside.

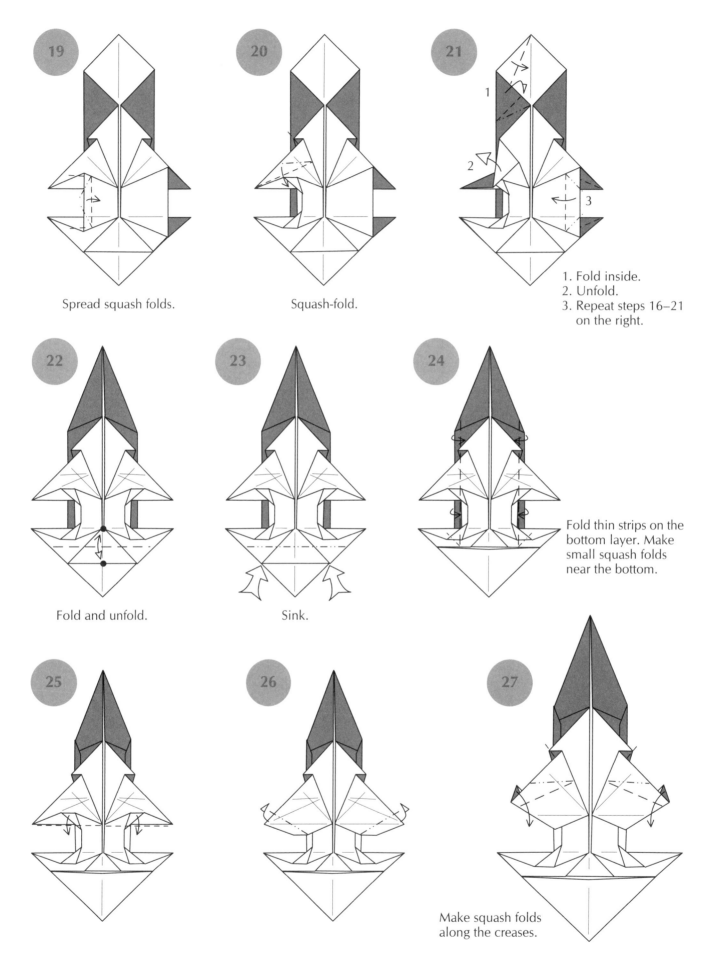

19 Spread squash folds.

20 Squash-fold.

21
1. Fold inside.
2. Unfold.
3. Repeat steps 16–21 on the right.

22 Fold and unfold.

23 Sink.

24 Fold thin strips on the bottom layer. Make small squash folds near the bottom.

25

26

27 Make squash folds along the creases.

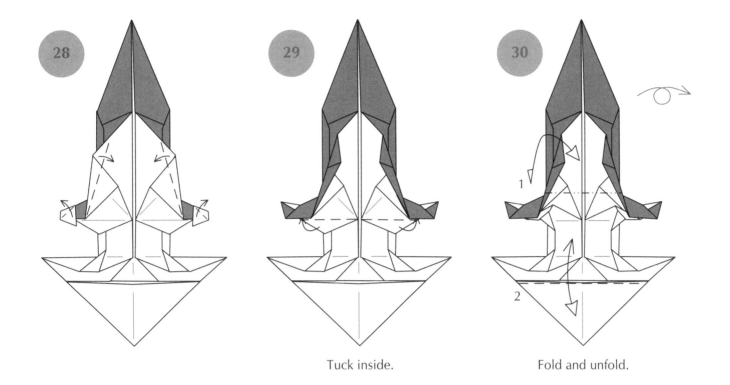

28

29

Tuck inside.

30

Fold and unfold.

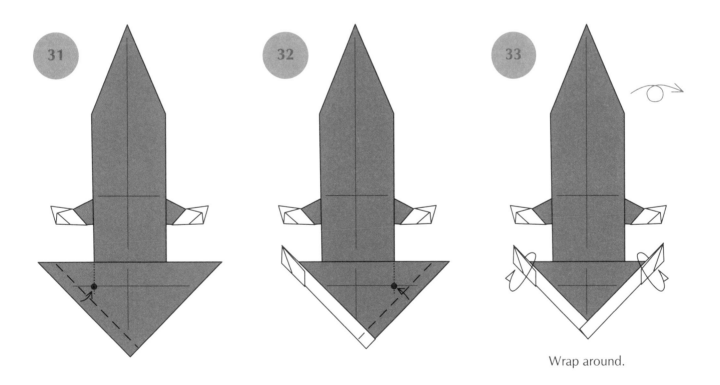

31

32

33

Wrap around.

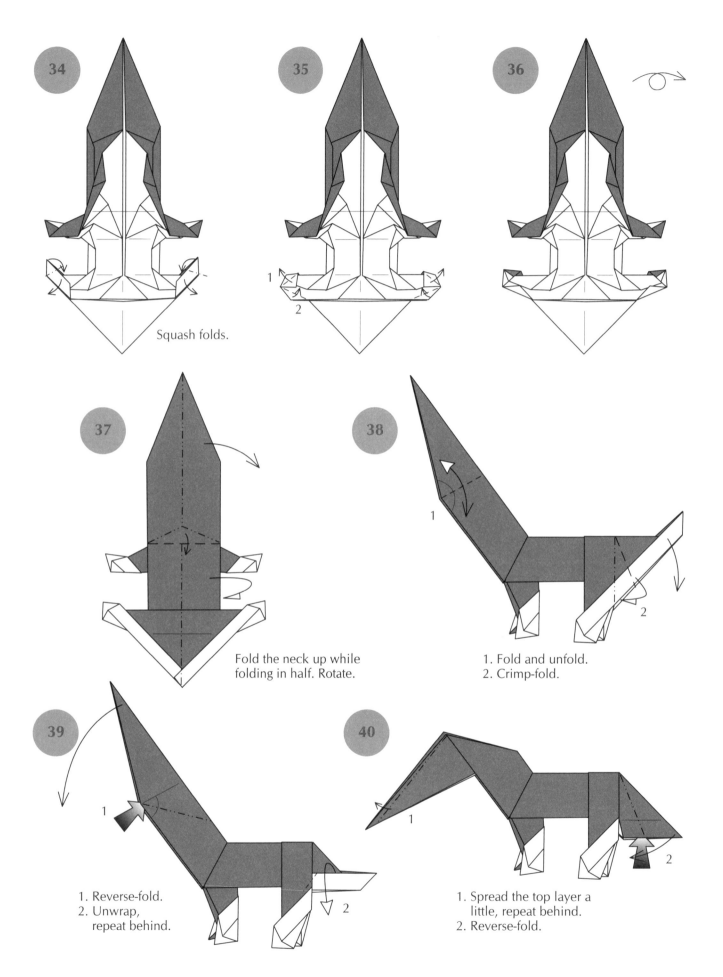

34

Squash folds.

35

1
2

36

37

Fold the neck up while folding in half. Rotate.

38

1. Fold and unfold.
2. Crimp-fold.

1
2

39

1. Reverse-fold.
2. Unwrap, repeat behind.

1
2

40

1. Spread the top layer a little, repeat behind.
2. Reverse-fold.

1
2

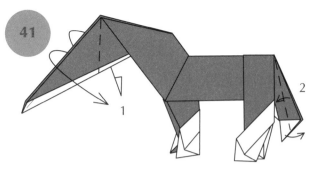

41

1. Outside-reverse-fold.
2. Repeat behind at the same time so the tail will swing out.

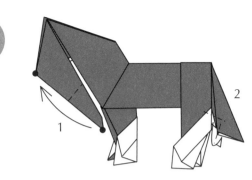

42

1. Outside-reverse-fold.
2. Reverse-fold inside the tail. Repeat behind.

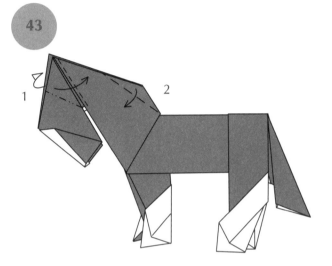

43

1. Crimp-fold.
2. Fold on one side.

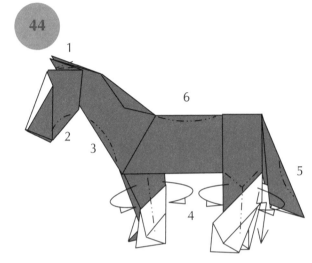

44

1. Shape the ears.
2. Shape the head.
3–6. Shape the neck, legs, tail, and back.
Repeat behind.

45

Clydesdale

Thoroughbred

Designed by John Montroll

A consummate racehorse, the Thoroughbred is prized for its speed and ability for high endurance activity. Agile and athletic, the Thoroughbred can be found on racetracks around the world, where people from all walks of life enjoy the "Sport of Kings".

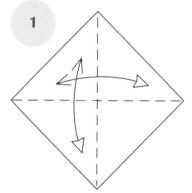

1

Fold and unfold.

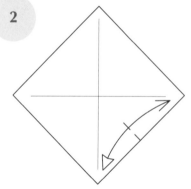

2

Fold and unfold on the bottom right.

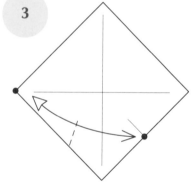

3

Fold and unfold on the left so the dots meet.

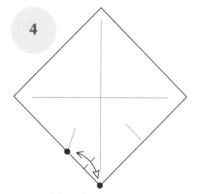

4

Fold and unfold on the left so the dots meet.

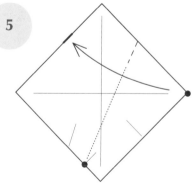

5

Bring the corner to the edge. Crease at the top.

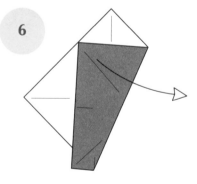

6

Unfold.

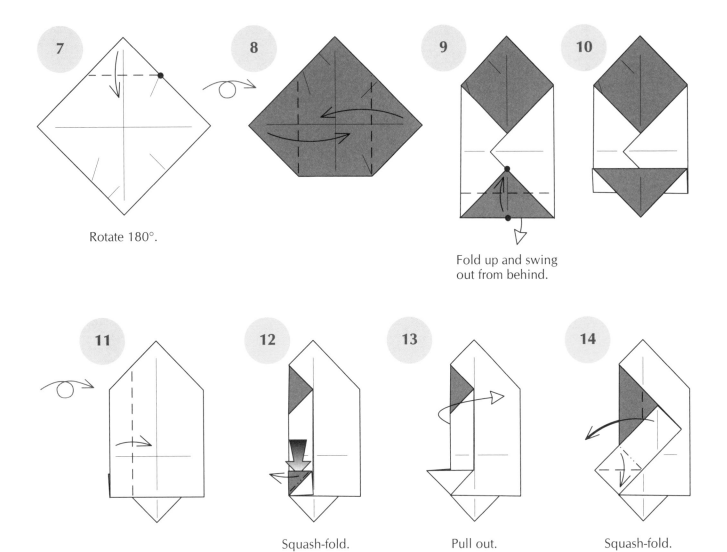

7 Rotate 180°.

8

9 Fold up and swing out from behind.

10

11

12 Squash-fold.

13 Pull out.

14 Squash-fold.

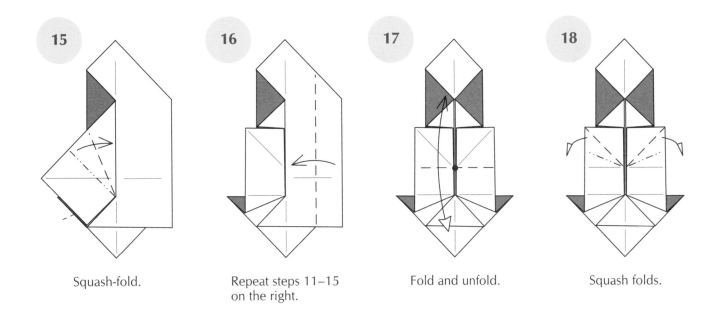

15 Squash-fold.

16 Repeat steps 11–15 on the right.

17 Fold and unfold.

18 Squash folds.

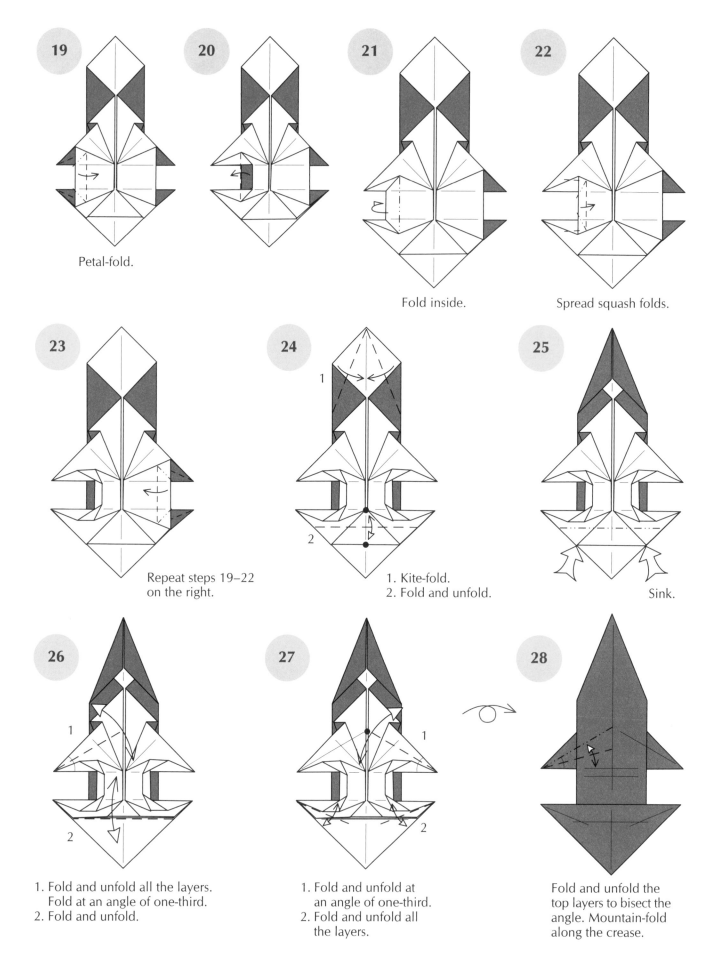

19

Petal-fold.

20

21

Fold inside.

22

Spread squash folds.

23

Repeat steps 19–22
on the right.

24

1. Kite-fold.
2. Fold and unfold.

25

Sink.

26

1. Fold and unfold all the layers.
   Fold at an angle of one-third.
2. Fold and unfold.

27

1. Fold and unfold at
   an angle of one-third.
2. Fold and unfold all
   the layers.

28

Fold and unfold the
top layers to bisect the
angle. Mountain-fold
along the crease.

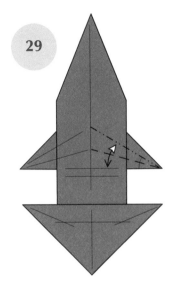

29

Fold and unfold.

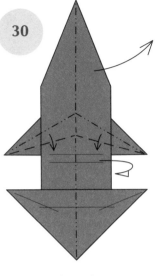

30

Fold along the creases and rotate.

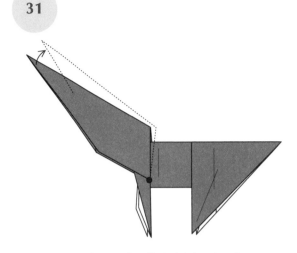

31

Pivot the neck a little bit by the dot.

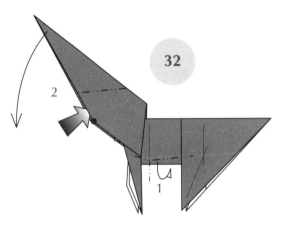

32

1. Fold inside and repeat behind.
2. Reverse-fold so the edge meets the dot.

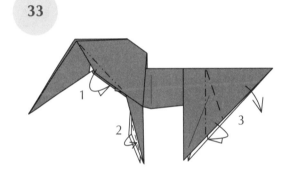

33

1. Fold inside, repeat behind.
2. Fold inside, repeat behind.
3. Crimp-fold.

34

1. Outside-reverse-fold.
2. Reverse-fold, repeat behind.

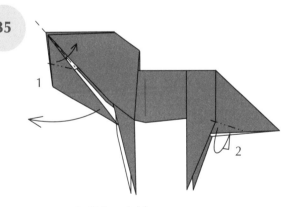

35

1. Crimp-fold.
2. Fold inside, repeat behind.

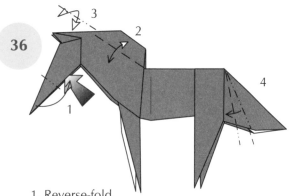

36

1. Reverse-fold.
2. Fold and unfold all the layers.
3. Fold and unfold all the layers behind along the same crease.
4. Crimp-fold.

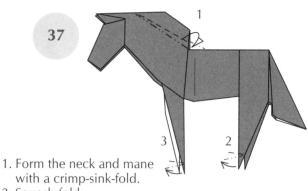

37

1. Form the neck and mane with a crimp-sink-fold.
2. Squash-fold.
3. Spread the tip.
Repeat behnd.

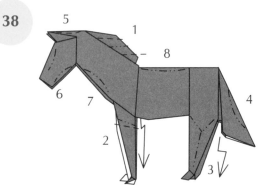

38

1. Pleat-fold the mane.
2. Crimp-fold.
3. Shape the legs.
4. Shape the tail.
5. Shape the ears.
6–8. Shape the head, neck, and back.

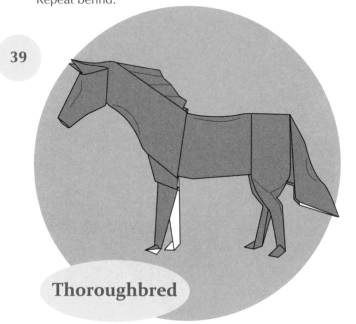

39

Thoroughbred

Galloping Thoroughbred

Begin with step 38 but:
1. Do not fold the tail in step 36.
2. Do not fold the hooves on the front legs in step 37.

1

Shape the front legs with crimp and reverse folds. Shape the hind legs and tail. Shape the neck, mane, head and back as in the standing model.

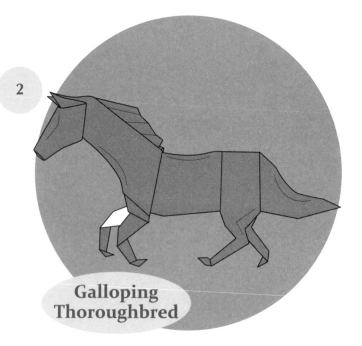

2

Galloping Thoroughbred

Mustang

Designed by John Montroll

North American Mustangs have earned a place in popular culture, even having a car named after them in celebration of their speed, endurance and love of wide open spaces. Originally from Spain, they can be found in rodeos and are a fine choice for trail riding.

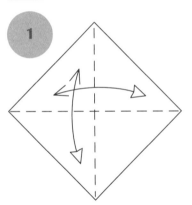

Fold and unfold.

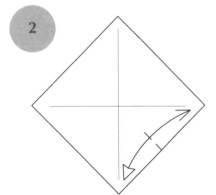

Fold and unfold on the bottom right.

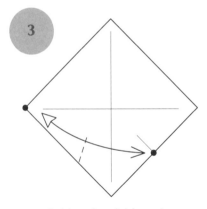

Fold and unfold on the left so the dots meet.

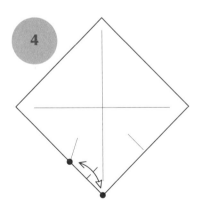

Fold and unfold on the left so the dots meet.

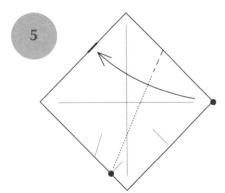

Bring the corner to the edge. Crease at the top.

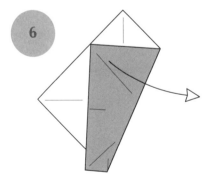

Unfold.

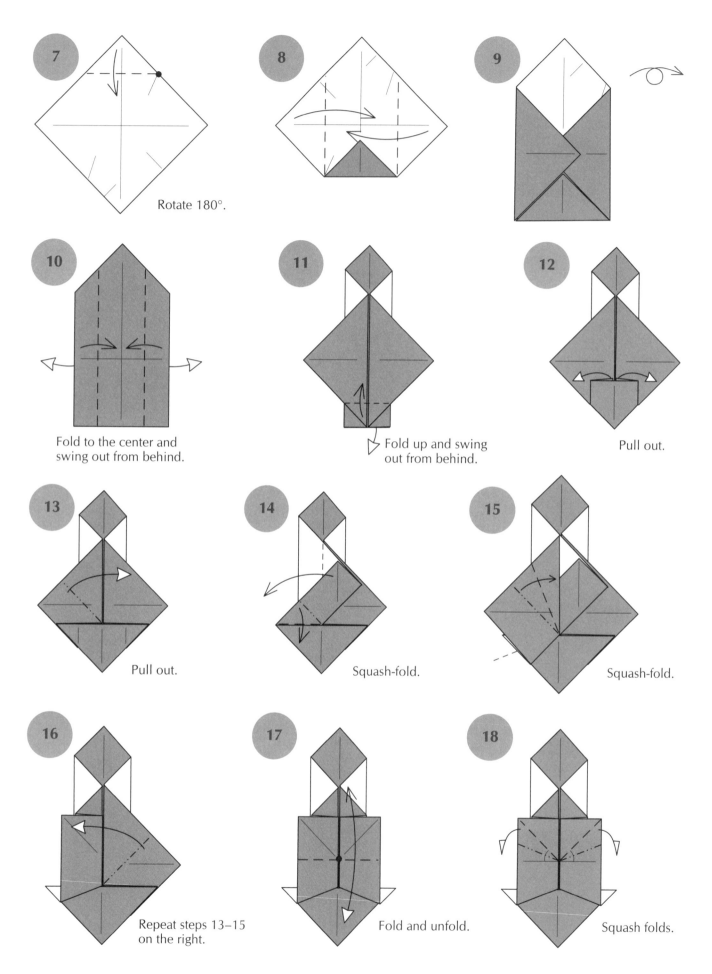

7 Rotate 180°.

8

9

10 Fold to the center and swing out from behind.

11 Fold up and swing out from behind.

12 Pull out.

13 Pull out.

14 Squash-fold.

15 Squash-fold.

16 Repeat steps 13–15 on the right.

17 Fold and unfold.

18 Squash folds.

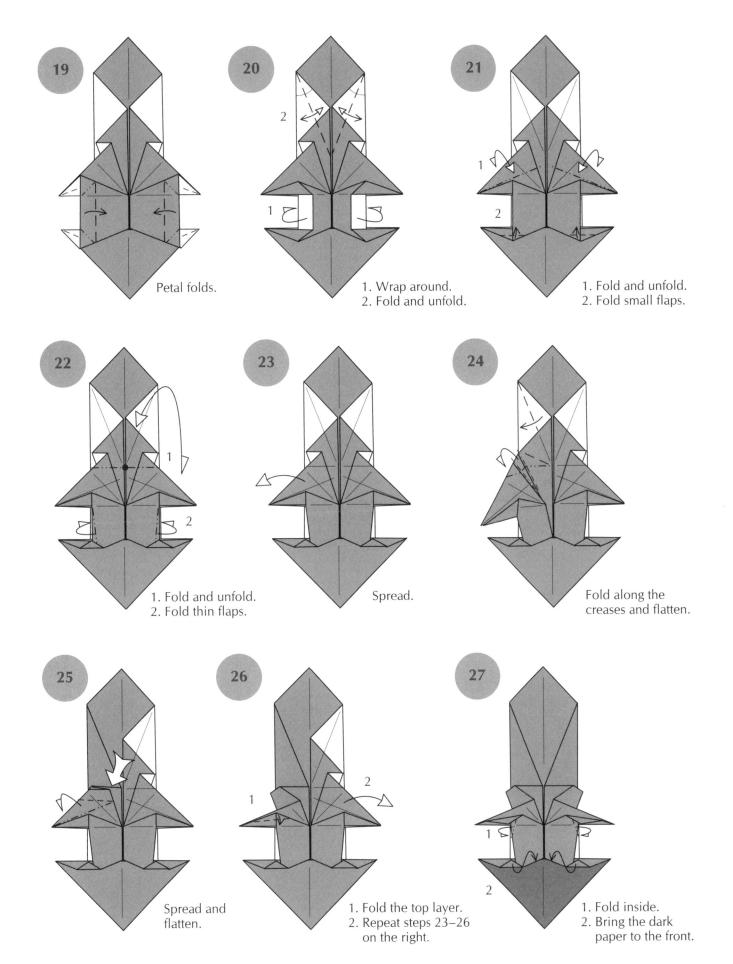

19 Petal folds.

20
1. Wrap around.
2. Fold and unfold.

21
1. Fold and unfold.
2. Fold small flaps.

22
1. Fold and unfold.
2. Fold thin flaps.

23 Spread.

24 Fold along the creases and flatten.

25 Spread and flatten.

26
1. Fold the top layer.
2. Repeat steps 23–26 on the right.

27
1. Fold inside.
2. Bring the dark paper to the front.

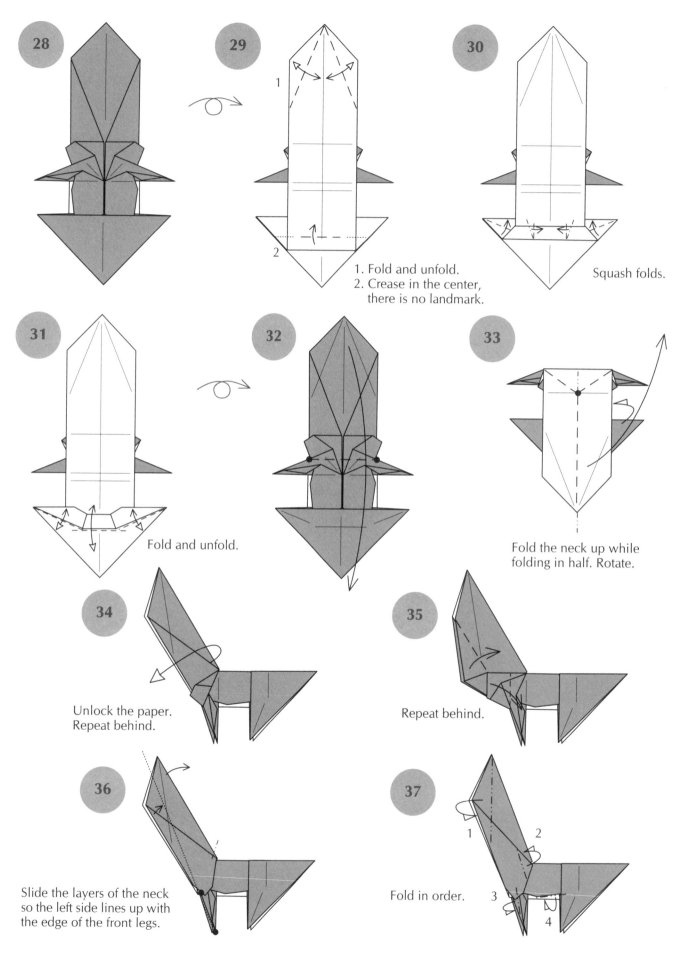

28

29

1. Fold and unfold.
2. Crease in the center,
   there is no landmark.

30

Squash folds.

31

Fold and unfold.

32

33

Fold the neck up while
folding in half. Rotate.

34

Unlock the paper.
Repeat behind.

35

Repeat behind.

36

Slide the layers of the neck
so the left side lines up with
the edge of the front legs.

37

Fold in order.

38

1. Reverse-fold.
2. Crimp-fold.

39

1. Spread the top layer.
2. Fold inside.
3. Fold inside.
Repeat behind.

40

1. Outside-reverse-fold.
2. Fold inside.
3. Fold inside.
4. Fold inside.
Repeat behind.

41

1. Crimp-fold.
2. Squash folds, repeat behind.

42

1. Reverse-fold.
2. Pleat-fold the mane.
3. Thin the legs, repeat behind.
4. Pleat-fold the tail.

43

1. Shape the head.
2. Shape the ears.
3. Shape the legs.
4. Crimp-fold.
5. Shape the back.
Repeat behind.

44

Mustang

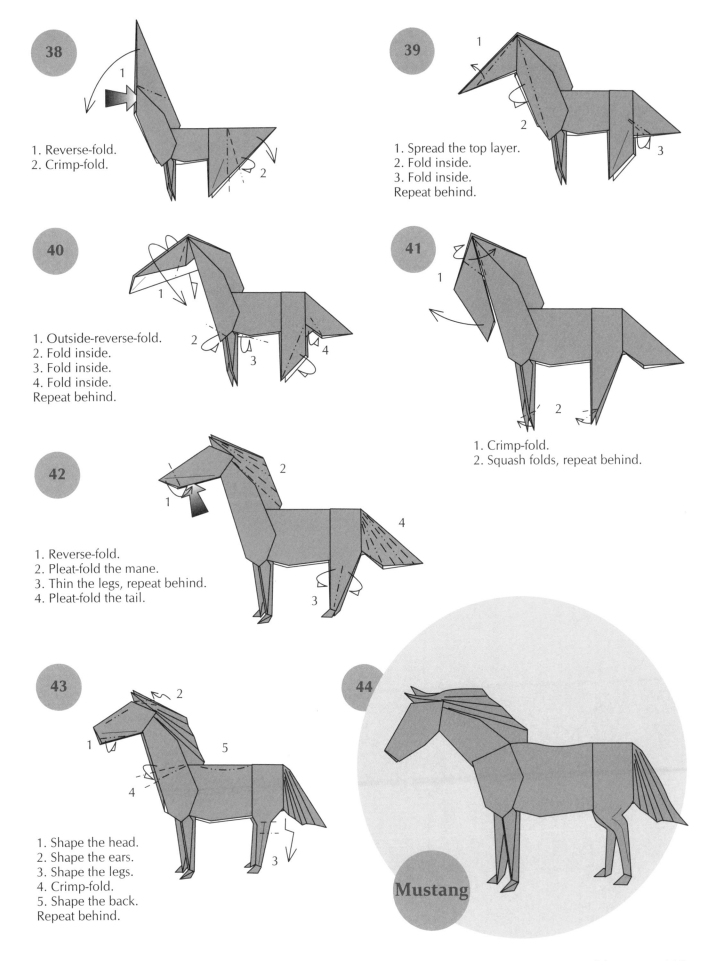

Arabian

Designed by John Montroll

Originally found on the Arabian Peninsula, these noble and intelligent horses are one of the most popular breeds of horses, and are prized for their ability to work well alongside humans. Gentle enough to live in desert tents with families and children, Arabian Horses have proven themselves throughout history as loyal creatures who would be equally at home in the ancient desert or in today's local parade or on a quiet country horse trail.

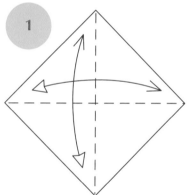

Fold and unfold.

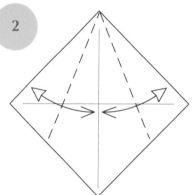

Kite-fold and unfold.

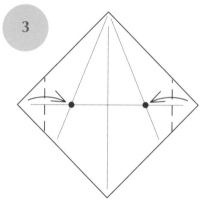

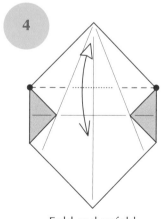

Fold and unfold
by the edges.

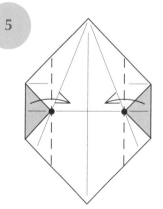

1. Squash folds.
2. Fold up.

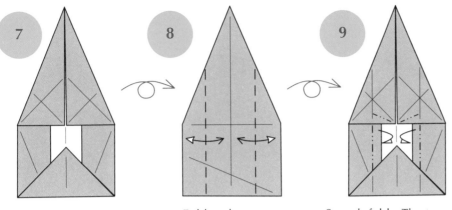
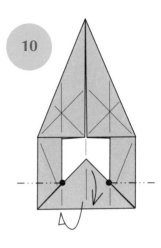

Fold to the center and unfold.

Squash folds. The two upper mountain fold lines are for hidden layers.

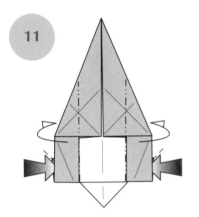
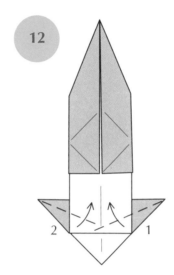
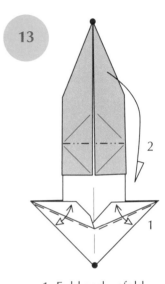

Reverse-folds.

Fold in order.

1. Fold and unfold.
2. Fold behind so the dots meet.

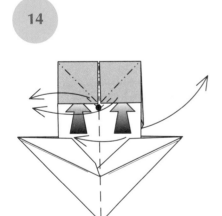
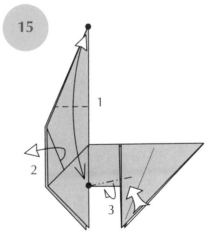
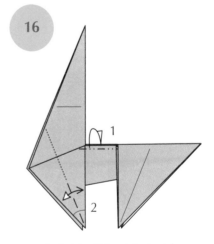

Push in at the dot and fold in half. Fold the neck up and the bring the front legs out. Rotate.

1. Fold and unfold.
2. Pull out.
3. Fold inside with a hidden reverse fold by the hind legs.
Repeat behind.

1. Fold a thin strip inside.
2. Fold and unfold.
Repeat behind.

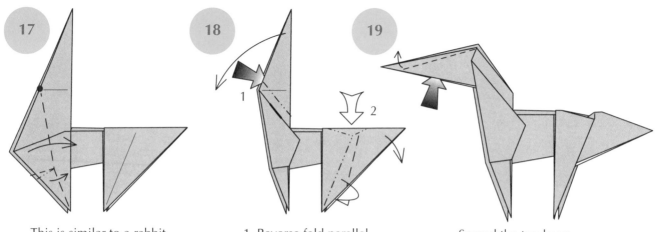

17

This is similar to a rabbit ear. Repeat behind.

18

1. Reverse-fold parallel to the bold line.
2. Push in at the top and make a crimp fold.

19

Spread the top layer. Repeat behind.

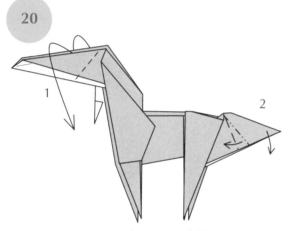

20

1. Outside-reverse-fold.
2. Crimp-fold.

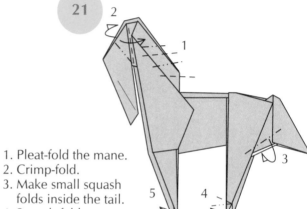

21

1. Pleat-fold the mane.
2. Crimp-fold.
3. Make small squash folds inside the tail.
4. Squash-fold.
5. Spread at the tip.
Repeat behind.

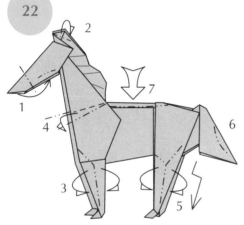

22

1. Reverse-fold.
2. Fold inside.
3. Thin the front legs.
4. Crimp-fold.
5. Thin and shape the hind legs.
6. Shape the tail.
7. Shape the back.
Repeat behind.

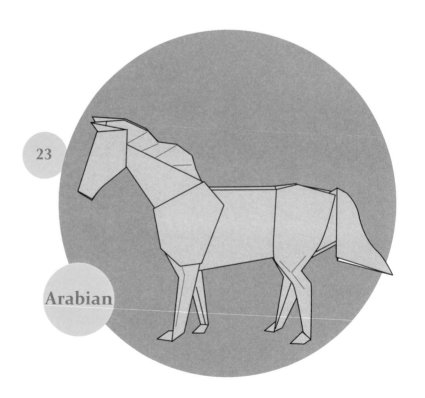

23

Arabian

Lipizzan

Designed by John Montroll

The Lipizzan Horse is known and admired the world over for its regal bearing and high-stepping gait. Descended from Arabian and Spanish stock, Lipizzans are gentle, easy to train, and are often featured in circuses and shows.

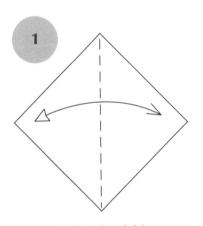

Fold and unfold.

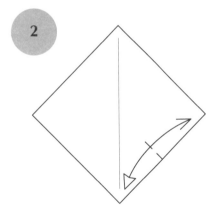

Fold and unfold on the edge.

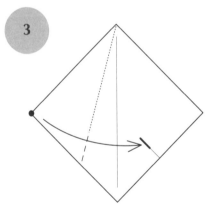

Bring the corner to the line.

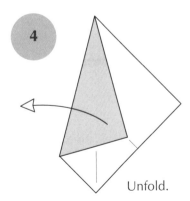

Unfold.

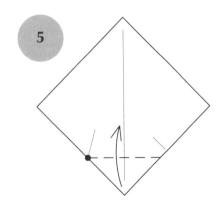

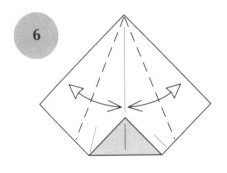

Kite-fold and unfold.

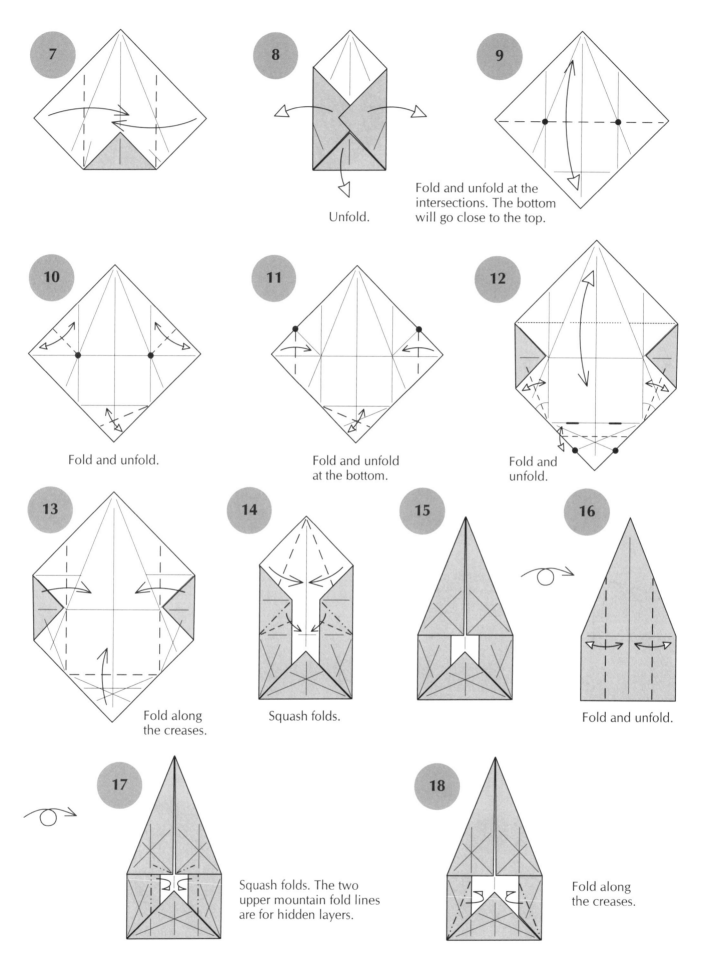

7

8 Unfold.

9 Fold and unfold at the intersections. The bottom will go close to the top.

10 Fold and unfold.

11 Fold and unfold at the bottom.

12 Fold and unfold.

13 Fold along the creases.

14 Squash folds.

15

16 Fold and unfold.

17 Squash folds. The two upper mountain fold lines are for hidden layers.

18 Fold along the creases.

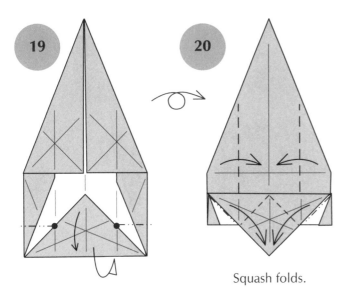

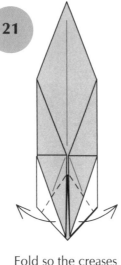

Squash folds.

Fold so the creases in the next step are on the same line.

Note the highlighted creases are on the same horizontal line. Unlock the paper.

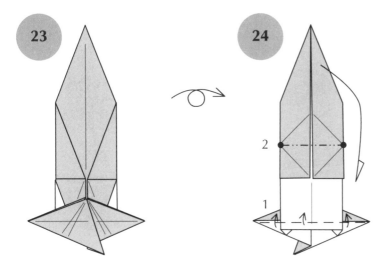

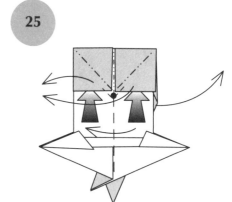

Push in at the dot and fold in half. Fold the neck up and the bring the front legs out. Rotate.

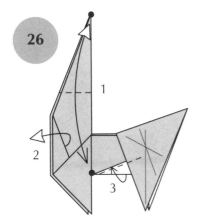

1. Fold and unfold.
2. Pull out.
3. Tuck inside.
Repeat behind.

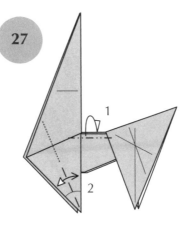

1. Fold a thin strip inside.
2. Fold and unfold.
Repeat behind.

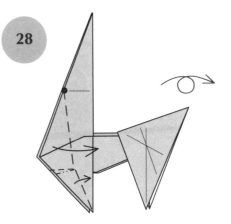

This is similar to a rabbit ear. Repeat behind.

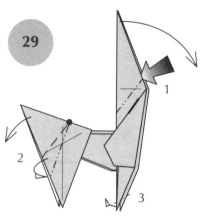

29

1. Reverse-fold parallel to the bold line.
2. Mountain-fold along the crease for this crimp fold.
3. Squash-fold behind.

30

1. Spread the top layer, repeat behind.
2. Fold behind, repeat behind.
3. Fold inside, repeat behind.
4. Fold to the right.

31

1. Outside-reverse-fold.
2. Fold inside, repeat behind.

32

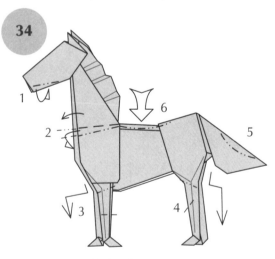

1. Fold inside, repeat behind.
2. Crimp-fold.
3. Squash-fold.
4. Squash-fold, repeat behind.

33

1. Reverse-fold.
2. Pleat-fold.
3. Crimp-fold.
4. Thin the legs, repeat behind.

34

1. Repeat behind.
2. Crimp-fold.
3. Shape the front leg.
4. Shape the hind legs, repeat behind.
5. Shape the tail.
6. Shape the back.

35

Lipizzan

Paint

Designed by John Montroll

Gentle and beautiful, the spotted Paint Horse is a multi-colored horse known for its gentleness to children and suitability for trail riding on horseback.

 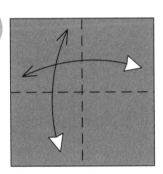 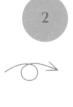 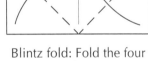  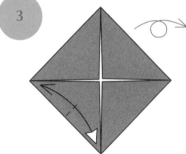

1 Fold and unfold.

2 Blintz fold: Fold the four corners to the center.

3 Fold and unfold on the edge.

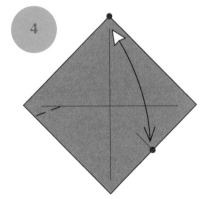  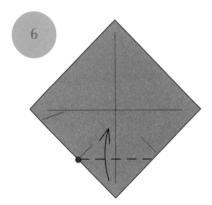

4 Fold and unfold on the left so the dots meet.

5 Fold and unfold on the left so the dots meet.

6

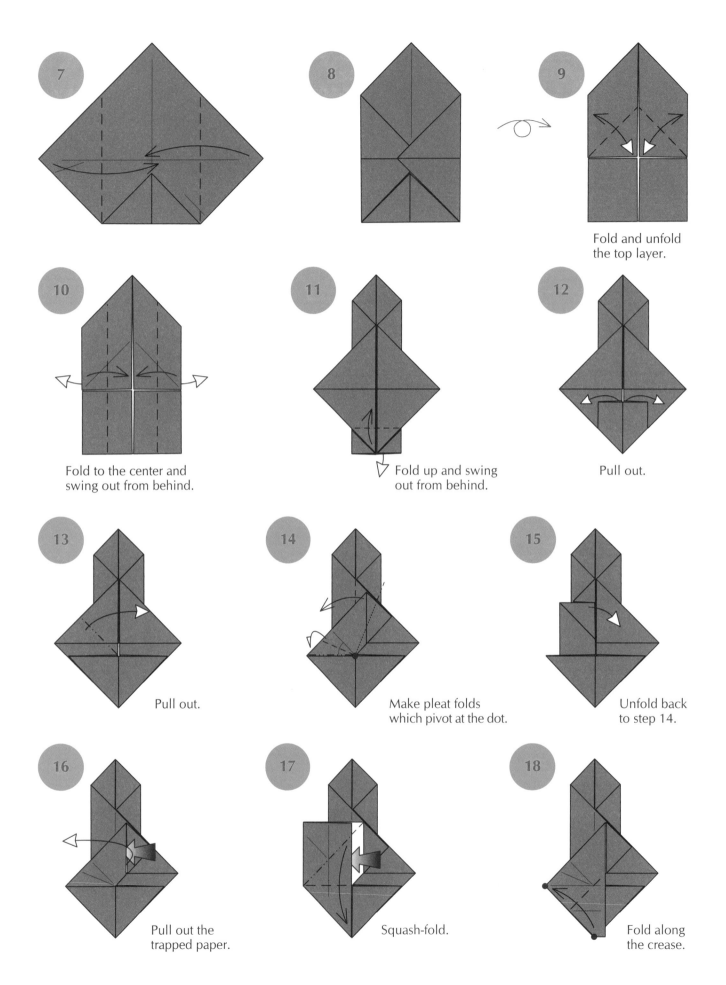

7

8

9

Fold and unfold
the top layer.

10

Fold to the center and
swing out from behind.

11

Fold up and swing
out from behind.

12

Pull out.

13

Pull out.

14

Make pleat folds
which pivot at the dot.

15

Unfold back
to step 14.

16

Pull out the
trapped paper.

17

Squash-fold.

18

Fold along
the crease.

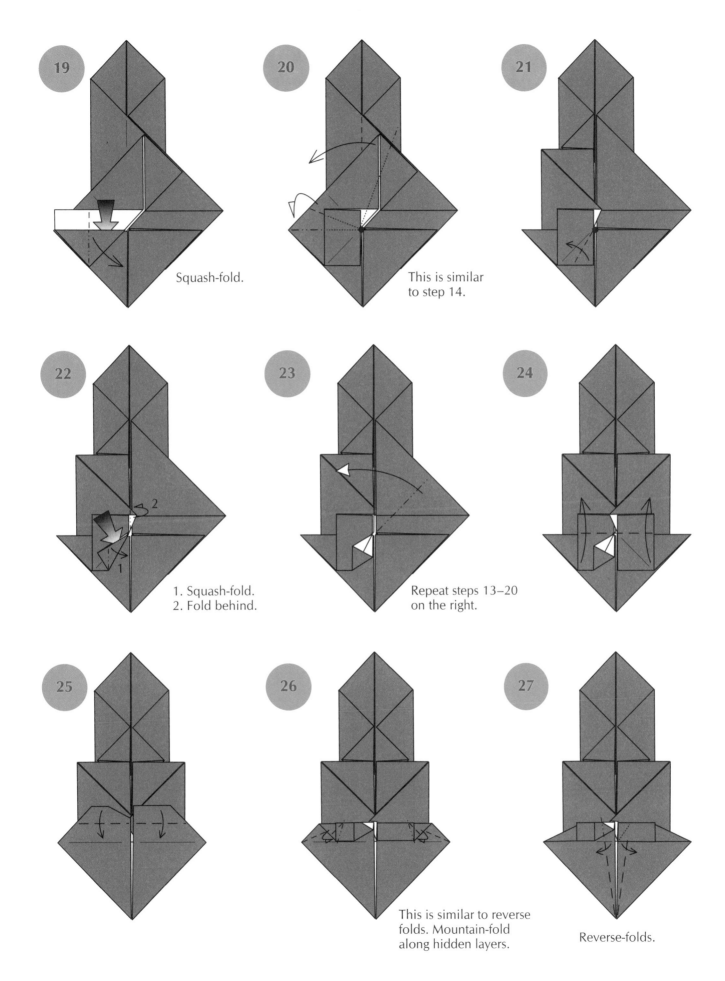

19 Squash-fold.

20 This is similar to step 14.

21

22 1. Squash-fold.
2. Fold behind.

23 Repeat steps 13–20 on the right.

24

25

26 This is similar to reverse folds. Mountain-fold along hidden layers.

27 Reverse-folds.

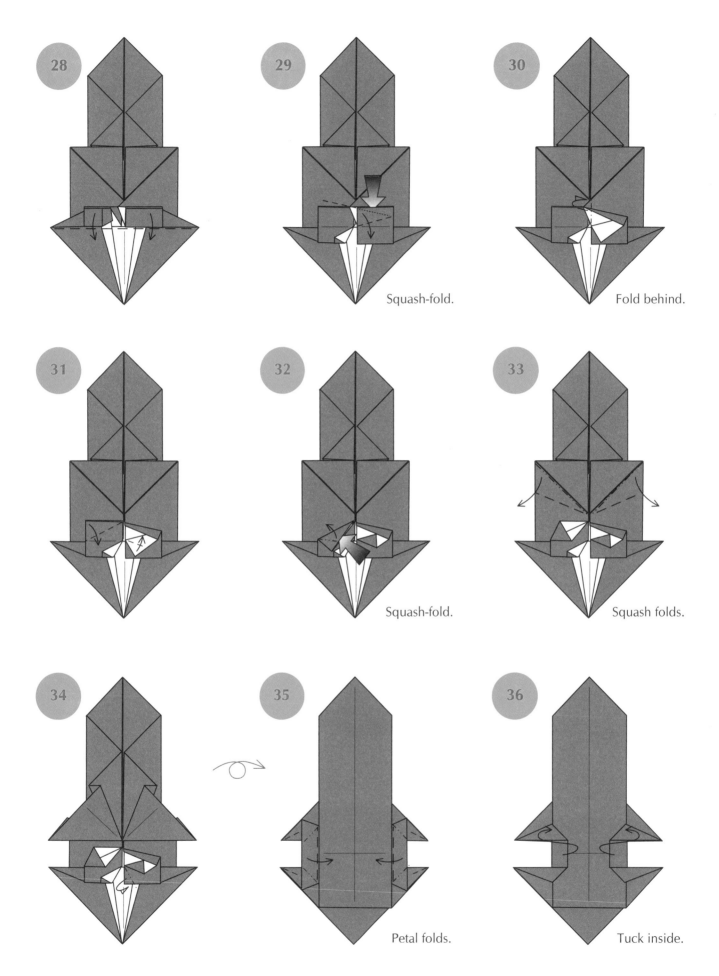

28

29 Squash-fold.

30 Fold behind.

31

32 Squash-fold.

33 Squash folds.

34

35 Petal folds.

36 Tuck inside.

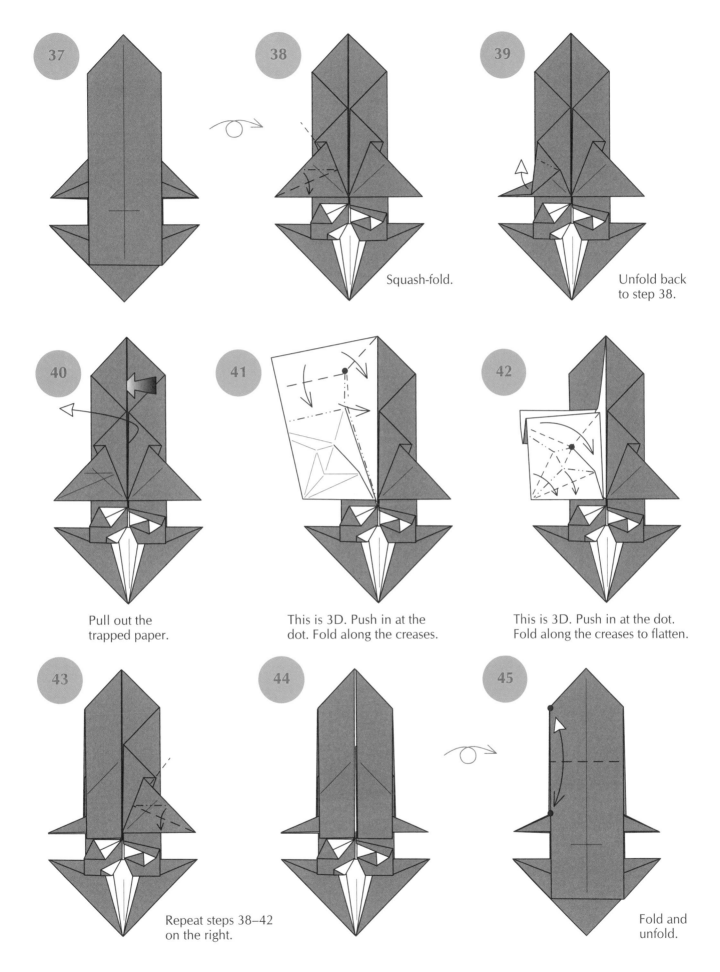

37

38 Squash-fold.

39 Unfold back to step 38.

40 Pull out the trapped paper.

41 This is 3D. Push in at the dot. Fold along the creases.

42 This is 3D. Push in at the dot. Fold along the creases to flatten.

43 Repeat steps 38–42 on the right.

44

45 Fold and unfold.

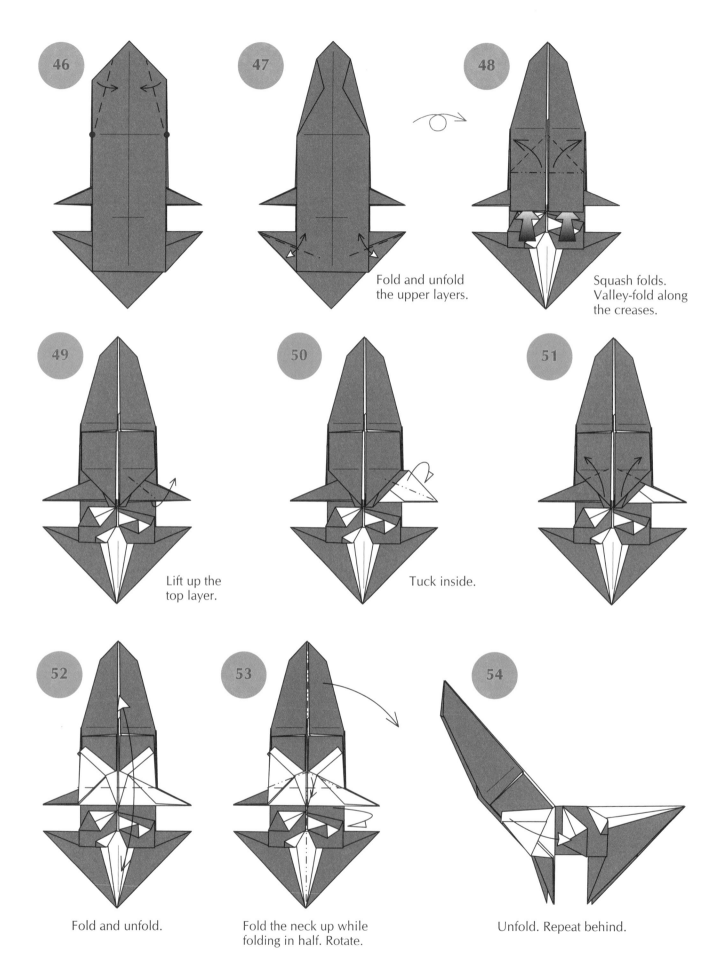

46

47

Fold and unfold
the upper layers.

48

Squash folds.
Valley-fold along
the creases.

49

Lift up the
top layer.

50

Tuck inside.

51

52

Fold and unfold.

53

Fold the neck up while
folding in half. Rotate.

54

Unfold. Repeat behind.

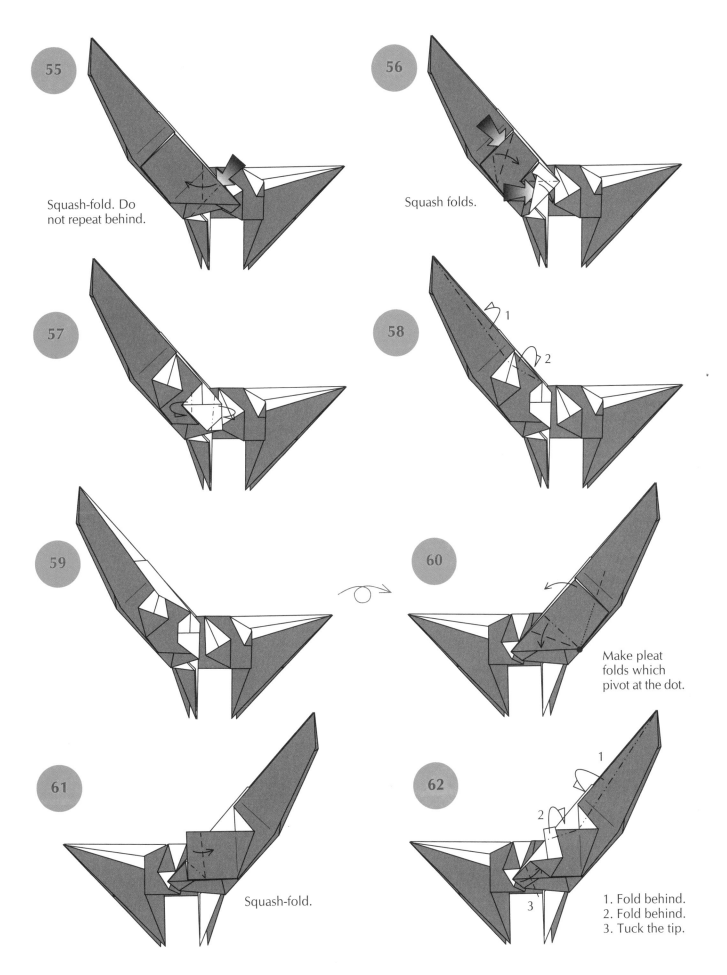

55 Squash-fold. Do not repeat behind.

56 Squash folds.

57

58
1
2

59

60 Make pleat folds which pivot at the dot.

61 Squash-fold.

62
1
2
3

1. Fold behind.
2. Fold behind.
3. Tuck the tip.

63

Reverse folds.

64

1. Fold inside.
2. Fold inside.
Repeat behind.

65

1. Outside-reverse-fold.
2. Repeat behind at the same time so the tail will swing out.

66

Crimp-fold.

67

Reverse-fold.

68

Shape the horse.

69

Paint

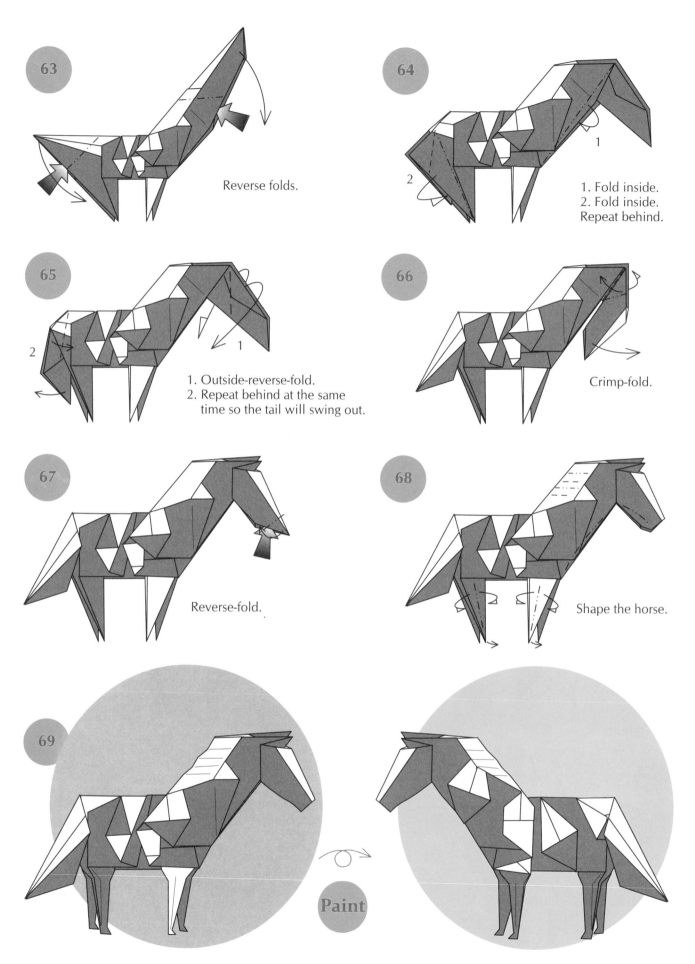